Stories of Self
Tracking children's identity and wellbeing through the school years

Stories of Self
Tracking children's identity and wellbeing through the school years

Jo Warin

A Trentham Book

Institute of Education Press, London

Institute of Education Press
20 Bedford Way
London
WC1H 0AL

First published 2010

British Library Cataloguing-in-Publication Data
A catalogue record for this book is available from the
British Library

ISBN 978 1 85856 441 8

Every effort has been made to acknowledge the source of
all material referred to in this book.

*Photographs by Dominque Hammond, Pete Johnson and
Arthur Thompson.*

Printed by CPI Group (UK) Ltd, Croydon, CR0 4YY

Contents

To Rowan, Jo, Harry and Jim

Acknowledgement

I want to say a very big thank-you to my family, friends, and colleagues who have supported this enterprise, some for a very long time. Firstly, I want to acknowledge the huge amounts of patient support from Pete who has helped throughout the study in innumerable ways and has provided a constant, reliable and incredibly generous form of assistance. I want to thank Harry and Jim too for their continuing love and patience whilst they have grown up alongside this project. Many thanks also to the people who have had a more formal role in the study, especially to Janine Muldoon who assisted so helpfully during the early secondary school phase, to Alice Jesmont who transcribed some of the interviews, and to Becs Hibbin who read through the first draft. I am also indebted to Gillian Klein at Trentham Books for her encouragement and her very careful editing. A special thank you must go to Trevor Blackwell for his support and especially for his meticulous proof reading. A number of people have commented on various Chapters and cheered me on from the sidelines. I am very grateful for their encouragement: Mike Reynolds, Pippa Warin and Robert Warin. Several colleagues have been particularly supportive by lightening some of my teaching and administrative duties during the final stages of writing this book. Jo Dickinson deserves a particularly special mention in this respect and I would like to thank Ann Marie Houghton and Angela Lovett too.

Above all I am indebted to Anna, David, Ghita, Jayne, Kelley, Liam, Martin, Shelley, Simon, and Umar. I am deeply grateful for the generosity and trust they have brought to their participation in this study over so many years.

Jo Warin
January 2010

Foreword

This book is both unusual and important.

Longitudinal, qualitative studies of children's experiences are hard to carry out and Jo Warin and her participants are to be congratulated on this exceptional accomplishment. To express the achievement in this way recognises mutual contributions and the relational trust which is the foundation of such work. And reading the book, one is drawn into the stories and identities of each child, and can appreciate some of the fascination of coming to know them even as they developed themselves. Among the many strengths of the book are its sensitivity, realism and openness – and recognition of holistic complexity. Despite its accessibility, there is a multifaceted appreciation of each 'journey of childhood'.

And yet the major theme of the book also stands out clearly. This concerns the way in which a sense of 'self' is created, over time, to provide identity and meaning as children grow, develop and approach adulthood. This sense of self is a product of social interaction and becomes a resource for both coping with and managing social experiences. This, then, is a study of the process of becoming a person, in the sense of developing understanding of oneself in relation to others. In demonstrating such processes, Warin undermines the individualised determinism which can weigh children down with expectations. She demonstrates the potential of agency and the capacity to create and renew a sense of self which is always there. Personal narratives thus remain open to further development as new social relations and circumstances are experienced.

In these ways, Jo Warin has made an exceptional contribution to our growing understanding of the enduring themes of learning and developing though the life-course.

Andrew Pollard

Section 1
Beginnings

Introduction

This is a book of stories and about stories. It is about the stories we tell each other about ourselves and the stories we tell ourselves about ourselves.
Kearney, 2003:x

This book presents and discusses the unique longitudinal case studies about five children whom I have talked with and observed from the ages of three to seventeen. In telling their stories my main focus is on their construction of a personal identity as they progress through their school lives. These stories illustrate ideas about the nature and function of identity, and feed current debates about the wellbeing of children and young people.

The book has a dual purpose:

- to illuminate journeys of childhood in order to help us as carers, teachers, parents and politicians to build up a much more detailed knowledge of children's lives than we currently have access to

- to bring a much needed grounded perspective to current debates about the importance of a personal identity, exploring how self is created over time.

Insights into children's lives

I seek to create a window into children's internal lives, providing a detailed view of intrapersonal development, showing change over the time-span of childhood and adolescence. The increase in the number and scope of child oriented professions, and the inter-professional collaboration between them, means that the range of people who need access to stories of children's lives has grown. A knowledge of children's interests, habits, language practices, temperament, emotional ups and downs, customs, family relationships and activities will greatly assist teachers and other child-focused professionals to be effective in their work. Yet the strategies and resources for enabling professionals to gain this kind of knowledge are surprisingly thin. Longitudinal case studies can provide us with insights into the detailed reality of children's lives. Significantly, they can also reveal change and how children themselves observe and comment on change. As they show children's lives unfolding over time, they also have the power to call into question some of the shibboleths of child development.

Generally, people who decide they want to enter child-focused professions such as teaching do so because they have had a reasonably positive experience of relating to children, but often this is minimal. Some are themselves parents and consequently have insight into their own children's lives. However such knowledge is limited and can lead to expectations of children that are blind to the wide variation of childhood experiences. So teachers who are parents also need to develop their inside knowledge of children's lives.

There are a number of reasons for stressing the significance of such knowledge. Firstly, such understanding is the cornerstone for the empathy with children and young people so essential for sensitive teaching and care. Secondly, it mitigates the rather crude assessments and measures such as CATs (cognitive ability tests) and SATs (standard assessment tests) that can come to represent individual pupils. Thirdly, when we deepen our knowledge of each individual in the classroom we are less likely to respond to them as if they were a stereotype. Fourthly, attempts to get to know children as fully as possible provide a basis for inclusion. Finally, the greater the inside knowledge a teacher has about a child, the better able they will be to communicate well with the parents. Good home-school knowledge exchange is both the means by which teachers can access such knowledge as well as the means by which they can make good use of it.

Insights into identity – from an interdisciplinary perspective
A secondary purpose of the book is to explore some fascinating and important questions about the meaning of 'self'. Do we need to construct an identity for ourselves? Does identity serve a useful purpose? Or is it a

deeply ingrained habit of thought that we would do well to escape? Researchers and theoreticians who attempt to find answers to these questions are not themselves outside of such thought habits and are likely to be influenced in their own search for answers by the academic disciplines with which they identify. A cognitive developmental psychologist would be more likely to accentuate the way that central aspects of self formed early during a person's life create a schematic structure that functions to categorise experience. A sociologist, perhaps influenced by Foucault's theories, would emphasise the way that the shifting power movements within a social group impact on the individual's experience of their subjectivity within that group. If we want to get outside of our own, blinkered, researcher identities that are shaped by the theories of specific academic disciplines we need to become more interdisciplinary.

The term 'interdisciplinary' reflects my own career as an academic working at the interface between sociology and psychology. Yet it also stretches back to an interest and involvement in theatre and in fictional literature. I worked out, early on in my life, that my enjoyment of fiction was about getting to know other characters as if from the inside, inhabiting their lives and trying to imagine how they felt. This impetus has driven the study presented in this book and continues to motivate an interest in identity, empathy and relational awareness, the concepts that underlie this book.

I have used my interactions with the children in the study to cast light on theories about the construction of identity. Simultaneously I have harnessed theories of identity to help me understand the children. When I began this study I was a newish parent. As such I was intrigued by psychologists who had studied their own children's development, for example Piaget and Freud. I didn't conduct a study of my own children for two reasons. Firstly, I believed that such research would not be objective, a misgiving I have since discarded as my understanding of research methodology has changed (as I discuss in Chapter 5). Secondly, I was much too deeply engaged with the actual practice and daily minutiae that is implicated in life with infants and young children. How many nappies did Piaget change, I wonder? My intention, as I set out to select a sample of children to study, was to create an empirical pool of experience to observe and reflect on, one that would be purer than the muddy waters of interactions with my own children, obscured by the intensity of my psychological and emotional relations with them.

Overview

The book is divided into three sections. 'Beginnings' – Chapters 1 to 5 – provides an account of the theoretical and political importance of concerns about the quality of childhood and child wellbeing, and the contribution of qualitative longitudinal research to these debates. Chapter 1 discusses the growing political emphasis on children and childhood that has arisen alongside a rapidly growing research interest in listening to the voices of children and exploring child wellbeing. This perspective suggests we need to know and understand children as people in their own right rather than as the raw materials for the adults we plan for them to become. In Chapter 2, I discuss the rarity of genuine longitudinal studies of children and reflect on psychological and sociological theories about their 'life-chances', for example the extent to which future outcomes are pre-determined by early childhood experiences.

Chapter 3 explores whether we need a 'self'. One answer to this question is that the development of a consistent sense of self, built up over time, is the bedrock of mental health. Another is that the self is an untenable concept which simply cannot capture the complexities and inconsistencies of real lives. I discuss why this question, and these very different answers, matter to policy makers and professionals concerned with the education and care of children and young people.

Chapter 4 concerns childhood and adolescence, including the role played by the social world of school, as a context for developing a sense of self. Chapter 5 tells the story of my relationship with the children over the years of the study. This was, initially, in a three year phase from the child's pre-school year to the end of their second year in primary school and then in a follow up phase of sequential visits between ages twelve to seventeen. I explain my selection of the original sample of ten pre-schoolers and my rationale for the five whose stories are presented. I discuss how my methods can best be characterised as intermittent, longitudinal ethnography and portray my researcher position as a witness of change. I also explore the ethical issues particular to this form of research.

In section two, 'Plots and sub plots. Matching theory with real lives: five stories of self through school', I present the narratives of Martin, Shelley, Simon, Jayne and Liam, following their lives from pre-school to the end of formal schooling, homing in on social and personal aspects of the making of identity and emphasising the educational importance of self awareness and awareness of others. Through Martin's story I speculate about the origins of his value for an authentic self which, I argue, constitutes 'identity capital', an advantageous capacity for self awareness. I reflect on the conditions for developing this. Shelley's story raises important issues about inconsistencies in behaviour between the social worlds of home and school and what this disparity means for the construction of self. In Simon's life, a critical moment, an assault, prompts a consideration of the pivotal role of key incidents as catalysts for telling a story of self. Jayne's story is one of ups and downs in her personal self confidence and her eventual attainment of a nuanced and adaptable identity. In Liam's story I look at the influence of social class on processes of self making, considering the argument that the production of identity is the prerogative of those with the time and space to engage with it.

'Endings', the third section, leaves the young people on the threshold of adulthood, speculating about their chances in the future and looking back on their experiences of school life. I draw together conclusions about the ways these five stories have illuminated theories of identity and I propose that schooling has a vital role to play in ensuring that all children have access to the resources and opportunities that enable them to tell their stories of self.

Conventions used in this book

Children. As I am discussing a period of the human lifespan from 3 to 17 years of age it is sometimes inappropriate to use the term 'children', yet 'children and young people' can be a mouthful . So sometimes I have used 'children' to cover the entire age span.

Identity and self. I use these two words synonymously, making use of both for the sake of variety.

Confidentiality. All names, of the children, their parents, siblings, friends, and teachers have been fictionalised. Names of institutions and places have also been changed. In a few cases, other identifying details have also been disguised to provide greater anonymity.

1
The childhood revolution

Children's Song
*We live in our own world,
A world that is too small
For you to stoop and enter
Even on hands and knees,
The adult subterfuge.
And though you probe and pry
With analytic eye,
And eavesdrop all our talk
With an amused look,
You cannot find the centre
Where we dance, where we play,
Where life is still asleep
Under the closed flower,
Under the smooth shell
Of eggs in the cupped nest
That mock the faded blue
Of your remoter heaven.*

R.S. Thomas

Introduction

An inside knowledge of children's lives, their interests, habits, language practices, emotional ups and downs, family relationships and activities, is of vital importance to the work of teachers and other child-focused professionals. The backdrop to this claim is the escalating political emphasis on children and childhood that has arisen alongside a rapidly growing research interest in listening to the voices of children. In 1990 James and Prout drew attention to what they termed a new paradigm in the sociology of childhood, 'a call for children to be understood as social actors shaping as well as shaped by their circumstances'. Several years later James, Jenks and Prout (1998) pointed out that 'childhood has moved to the forefront of personal, political and academic agendas', claiming this to be a global movement, not just a Western one. This recent shift, reflected in both government policy and academic research, can be described as a slow revolution in that it represents a significant, though gradual, turn around in the ways we conceptualise the child and childhood, and in the amount of government attention currently being devoted to child wellbeing. The mood is captured in Brooks' (2006) prediction that 'the most exciting ideological battles of this century' will concern the nature of childhood and the needs and rights of children. How has this gradual revolution come about? I examine this firstly by looking at the increasing political emphasis on children and childhood, secondly by noting the escalation of academic discussion concerning the nature of childhood, and thirdly by revealing the growing attention to children's voices.

The politicisation of childhood

A concern with children's rights and power became a major constituent of the growing number of childhood studies programmes in higher education during the nineties. Oakley (1994) compares the growth of such programmes to the preceding growth in women's studies, drawing a parallel between the positioning of both women and children as a 'minority'. She suggests that the development of these specialist academic studies poses interesting political questions about the relationship between women and children as social minority groups and their positioning as objects of academic scrutiny. The term 'minority' in this debate is not intended to suggest the scarcity of children as a group but their limited power. James, Jenks and Prout (1998) support this argument and suggest it derives from its 'dedication to children's interests and purposes', creating, they say 'a sociology for rather than of children' (p31). This recent emphasis on children's power and rights of children has led to a politicisation of childhood.

As a political cause the wellbeing of children is undeniably worthy and so lends itself to becoming a political football. Since New Labour came to power in 1997 there has been a huge increase in child focused policy and legislation. Broadhurst *et al* (2009) describe an unremitting stream of legislative and organisational changes aimed at the related policy targets of children and families. Foley claims that child wellbeing has now risen to the top of the political agenda (2008). This has been accompanied by an increasing cacophony of media noise on the subject of children and childhood. In their recent inquiry into the quality of childhood, Layard and Dunn (2009) suggest that the high participation of contributors (35,000) reflects how strongly the subject of childhood resonates with people at this time.

Taking a global perspective on the tide of interest in childhood, the United Nations Convention on the Rights of the Child is a good place to start. Adopted by the United Nations member states in 1989 and made legally binding in 1990 (not yet ratified by USA), the convention spells out core principles of non-discrimination: devotion to the best interests of the child; the right to life, survival and development; and respect for the views of the child (UNICEF, 2009). This was a landmark in the momentum of global interest in the rights and needs of children and in the nature of childhood. In the same year, 1989, in the UK the Children Act became law, marking a significant step towards acting on the last of the UNICEF principles with regard to 'the ascertainable wishes and feelings of the child' in family battles over child custody. This statement marked a radical move towards the need to listen to children and take seriously what they say. In the late nineties, child-directed policy in the UK became focused on the early years of childhood as the government laid the foundations for the Sure Start programme.

However, whilst there has been a torrent of child focused policy-making within the New Labour government, this has not been unambiguously focused on the wellbeing of children. Sure Start was designed to hit several policy targets in one fell swoop, including adult employment. The welfare to work programme, intended to enable parents to participate fully in the workforce, partly to reduce child poverty, prompted the need for a better system of childcare. Early critics of New Labour's childcare policy were aware of the mixed agendas. A respondent to the 'Meeting the Childcare Challenge' consultation (DfEE, 1998) advised that 'Care needs to be taken to avoid putting too much emphasis on the link between childcare and work at the expense of the child'. Sure Start was based on the widely applauded USA programme Head Start, an early intervention in education and care, introduced in 1965 to meet the needs of socially disadvantaged pre-schoolers in order to prevent later social deprivation, as a form of social investment. New Labour also believed in the social investment state which positions the child as the worker of the future. So policies aimed at children, whilst appearing to be directed at improving the quality of the children's lives were also clearly intended to develop the workers of the future, so creating a 'double dividend' . The Comprehensive Spending Review of 1998 portrayed Sure Start as a means of enhancing 'child and family development' whilst simultaneously leading to 'long term benefits for the exchequer' (Glass, 1999:261). Critics of New Labour's child policies have pointed out that benefits to children themselves can end up taking second place (Harding, 2000; Gewirtz, 2001, 2008; Williams, 2004; Warin 2007; Broadhurst *et al*, 2009).

Just as the Sure Start programme was influenced by Head Start in the USA, so the UK *Every Child Matters* (ECM) legislation in 2003 was in part influenced by the American *No Child Left Behind Act* of 2001, especially with regard to the egalitarian rhetoric of the title. The Act set out the need for every child to: Be healthy, Stay safe, Enjoy and achieve, Make a positive contribution, and Achieve economic wellbeing. Of particular relevance to this Chapter's focus on the rising tide of concern with the voice of children and young people, this legislation also stipulates that young people themselves should become part of any process of inspecting and evaluating the newly emerging children's services. A Children's Commissioner, Sir Al Aynsley Green, was appointed in England in 2005 in order to put this aim into practice and to ensure compliance with the United Nations convention of the Rights of the Child. Wales, Scotland and Northern Ireland now also have children's commissioners. In the UK there has been a Children's Minister since 2001. The change in UK government departments in 2007 gave prominence to children's issues with the creation of the Department for Children, Schools and Families (DCSF).

Every Child Matters was, in part, a response to the high profile case of Victoria Climbié, a child who was killed by her guardians in London in

2000. This sparked off a concern with child protection and, in particular, a concern with children 'falling through the cracks' of children's services and suggested the need for improved collaboration and communication between the different children's agencies. Sadly but inevitably, there have been further cases of serious child abuse and in 2009 the case of Baby P hit the UK headlines. Baby P was a seventeen month old child who lived in the same London borough as Victoria Climbié. He died from 50 injuries that had been inflicted over an eight month period during which time he had been repeatedly seen by social services. The *Every Child Matters* ideology of inter-professional collaboration has been criticised in some quarters as being an impossibility because of clashes between differing professional cultural values (Anning, 2005; Easen *et al,* 2000). However, more recently the concept of the 'team around the child' has evolved (Siraj-Blatchford *et al,* 2007) to portray the ideal of multi-agency working, to clarify what this means in practice and ensure that children are the focus of this collaboration.

When political and economic goals are at stake, it is the future value of children that is given prominence and this approach undermines their value as people in their own right, in the present moment (Burman, 2008; Guldberg, 2009). Getting underneath assumptions about the ways that childhood is valued necessitates a more detailed examination of how childhood has changed in its meanings during history and how it changes in different cultural contexts across the world.

The theorisation of childhood

Another aspect of the childhood revolution is the way the concept of childhood has been theorised during the last two to three decades. It has become the focus for much discussion about what this phase of life means, and how it is both distinct from and continuous with adulthood. Historians of childhood and childcare such as Aries (1973), Postman (1994) and Hardyment (1983) show us that the ways in which we have understood the very idea of childhood, and the meanings and values we attribute to it, have been influenced by the historical period. Aries for example tells us that in the middle ages there was no recognition of childhood as a separate phase of life, whilst Guldberg (2009) dates our current understanding of childhood as a discrete phase of the lifespan to the introduction of compulsory schooling in 1880, which created the idea that children were in a phase of 'becoming' adults, and entrenched the distinction between children and adults. Taken together, this work has led to the view that childhood is a fairly recent phenomenon. However, James, Jenks and Prout (1998) say that we need to be careful about this claim. It is not that childhood is a modern concept lacked by previous societies, but that previous societies lacked *our* concept. Childhood, they point out, is a relative concept, one that changes according to the values and purposes of the people discussing it at any one time.

Whilst a look back through history helps us to recognise that childhood is socially constructed, a look across the globe and into other cultures can also help us to look more critically at current Western assumptions about childhood. Maybin and Woodhead (2003) show the varied ways children are perceived and positioned within different societies, by contrasting the daily lives of children in Bangladesh, USA and South Africa. They reveal the limitations of our knowledge of Western childhoods and expose our assumptions that these are the same the world over. For example, they present different cultural accounts of pubertal rites of passage and the transition from childhoods into adulthoods. They conclude that there are often instances where the ideal type of 'independent' adult versus 'dependent' child doesn't fit the reality of people's lives (see also Rogoff, 2003). This very different approach to the meanings of 'child' and 'adult' reveals our implicit definitions of these constructs.

In 2007 the general public in the UK had childhood thrust under their noses and the smell was not a good one. UNICEF (United Nations Children's Fund) published a report comparing childhood wellbeing in 21 'rich' (industrialised) countries. The study used a framework of six dimensions of child wellbeing: material wellbeing, health and safety, educational wellbeing, family and peer relationships, behaviours and risks, and subjective wellbeing. The headline news for parents, policy makers and children in the UK was that our children seemed to be faring especially badly. The UK ranked 17th for educational wellbeing, a surprising 18th for material wellbeing, a disappointing 20th for subjective well being and an even worse 21st ranking for family and peer relationships and also for behaviours and risks. The report opens with the lines

> The true measure of a nation's standing is how well it attends to its children – their health and safety, their material security, their education and socialization, and their sense of being loved, valued, and included in the families and societies into which they are born.

These findings were disturbing for anybody concerned with child wellbeing in the UK, indicating a failure according to this 'true measure'. The report claims that 'such comparisons demonstrate that given levels of child wellbeing are not inevitable but policy-susceptible', so we can make changes to improve the quality of childhood if we can only recognise where policy is going wrong. The comparative data drawn together in the UNICEF report can operate as a prompt for the discussion and development of policies to improve children's lives.

A significant finding – perhaps the main key message of this report – was that children's subjective wellbeing, their happiness, is not explained or accounted for by their wealth (material wellbeing). This finding mirrors others that demonstrate that the equation between wealth and happiness is far from simple (Layard, 2005). This key message is also a significant one in *The Good Childhood Inquiry* by Layard and Dunn, another report that hit the UK media spotlight when it appeared in 2009. Launched in 2006 as a follow up to the Every Child Matters policy agenda, one of the main arguments is that an 'excessive individualism' in the wider society creates a competitive culture in which adults strive for independent personal success at the expense of family life and concern for dependent children. This attack on individualism is revisited in Chapter 3, since the ideal of 'making the most of yourself' that is attacked by Layard and Dunn raises important questions about how we conceptualise the 'self'. Taken together these two landmark reports, much discussed in the UK media, have created an idea that self-centred adults undermine the quality of children's lives.

The Good Childhood Inquiry was committed to gathering data from children themselves and devised strategies for accessing their views, for example in the form of 'my life' postcards. The inquiry claims to have received contributions from over 30,000 children and young people, adults and professionals. This brings me to a discussion of the third element of the 'childhood revolution', the emphasis in research and policy-making on children's voice.

The representation of childhood: children's voices

A significant strand of the growing phenomenon I have portrayed as a childhood revolution is a developing commitment to hearing children's own views on the matters that most closely affect their lives. It is now customary for policy-makers, academics, researchers and the professionals who work with children to prescribe the need to listen more attentively to them, a need that begins from the moment of birth. For example Mary John (2003) refers to the pioneering work of the French obstetrician Leboyer, whose approach to childbirth during the seventies emphasised the personhood of the newborn baby and the baby's eloquence in voicing their experience. She quotes the following lines from Leboyer: 'So can we say that a new born baby does not speak? No. It is we who do not listen' (John, 2003:28).

A growing number of academic studies have made a plea to listen to the voices of children. In their portrayal of the new paradigm for the sociology of childhood, Prout and James (1997) say that 'The history of the study of childhood in the social sciences has been marked not by an absence of interest in children but by their silence' (p7). They contrast the silence of children themselves with the massive corpus of knowledge about the child built up from the systematic studies of psychologists and social scientists. Only recently have researchers attempted to meet the challenge of engaging with children to amplify their voices.

The last decade has seen a huge rise in the number of books about the use of research methods with children (Christensen and James, 1999; Lewis and Lindsay, 1999; Woodhead and Faulkner, 2000; Lewis *et al*, 2004; Greene and Hogan, 2005.) A theme within many is the need to reverse the traditional approach to children as the objects of research and begin to position them as fellow researchers. Woodhead and Faulkner (2000) for example characterise this reversal as a change from working on children to working with children. This move comes about through a critique of traditional methods within psychology, particularly developmental psychology.

Burman's significant contribution to this debate (2008) has been to expose the taken-for-granted and dominant nature of the field of developmental psychology and reveal how children have been positioned within it as objects of enquiry. This approach, she points out, has led to a homogenisation of children and childhood, and a failure to recognise the variety of their pathways and the socio-cultural contexts they inhabit. In similar vein, Woodhead and Faulkner (2000) say 'Child Development is a body of knowledge constructed by adults for other adults to use in order to make sense of, regulate and promote children's lives and learning ...The research product is data interpreted in terms of adult discourses about children's development' (Woodhead and Faulkner, 2000:11-12). The logical extension of this critique is that children themselves should be trained as researchers. This is the approach that has been taken on board by researchers working with children at the Open University in the Children's Research Centre (CRC), where the aim is to empower children and enable them to undertake research projects – not on subjects chosen by adults, but on topics that are important to the youngsters themselves (Kellett, 2005).

Consulting children has also increasingly become practice within national government and local authorities in the UK. For example, the government consultation paper (Green paper) *Youth Matters* (2005) claims proudly that 19,000 young people responded, mainly through questionnaires sent to schools and youth organisations. In 2005 the Children's Rights Director, Roger Morgan, set up a unique children's conference at Legoland, Windsor (Morgan, 2005), where 700 children were invited to produce ideas about the five *Every Child Matters* outcomes. The event was organised specifically to include the voices of children aged 12 and under who, Morgan claims, don't usually respond to government consultation exercises. The report itself is written so as to be accessible to children. Morgan claims to have written 'only what the children told us at Legoland, not what we think as adults or what other people have said they think' (p5).

This is a laudable intention but as Burman (2008) points out, such good intentions to give children voice can mask the power gaps that exist between children and researchers. Clearly such exercises can be seen as rhetorical devices for gathering persuasive evidence to support government policies. Interestingly, a few of the children themselves, quoted by Morgan, showed some skepticism about this event. Burman suggests that we should be mindful about whose voice is being privileged in accounts that purport to represent children's voices. Her warning clearly applies to this book, and to my own relationship with the children whose words are included here.

Conclusion
The value of childhood: Threats and opportunities

Are we interested in children's wellbeing because we see this as an investment for the future, or because we are interested in children's happiness in the present moment? The seductive rhetoric of joined-up-thinking suggests these goals can be harmonious. But they are not always. Reducing child poverty has been a major policy goal, and parental participation in the workforce has been promoted as the means by which to achieve it. Whilst this is vitally necessary, it may be that the resulting poor work-life balance badly affects the quality of attention parents are able to give their children. Interestingly, in the Legoland exercise, Morgan found that children themselves place 'having enough money' at the bottom of the five goals for ECM. Whist his finding needs to be treated cautiously, since children's understandings about wealth and income are inevitably limited, it is revealing, the more so when put together with a research finding from Brannen *et al* (2000), who consulted children about parental work-life balance and found children's preferred model was part time work shared between two parents. So, paradoxically, the goal of improving children's material wellbeing through greater parental employment may threaten the quality of the parent-child relationship through the unavailability of the parents.

Investing in children for the adults they are to become undermines the quality of childhood in various ways. For example Guldberg (2009) points out that New Labour's 'excessive reliance on targets as a measure of success' leads to 'hothousing' children in nurseries, through the use of materials designed for anxious parents, for example Baby Einstein. Such programmes seduce parents into believing their young children can get ahead with a competitive advantage in the race to build up qualifications and eventual well paid forms of employment. Gewirtz (2008) goes one step further, showing that even the unborn foetus is subjected to forms of hothousing. Similarly, the misguided belief that an early start to the race for academic qualifications develops more winners has led to children in the UK starting formal schooling earlier than their European counterparts. These targets for children erode time for unstructured child oriented activities and play (Guldberg, 2009). There is significant tension, then, between the valuing of childhood per se and the valuing of childhood as the political means to achieving economic advantage through a high level of qualification and high employment.

The threats posed by undermining policy goals are matched by corresponding theoretical approaches to childhood that emphasise investment in the child for the adult they are to become. Burman (2008) shows that traditional approaches to developmental psychology position the child in this way. This radical shift of emphasis is connected to the dismantling of another shibboleth in traditional developmental psychology: the idea that early experiences in childhood and infancy have a formative influence on later experience – a point addressed in the next chapter. Developmental psychology focuses on the experiences of young children so that psychological interventions can be made in order to create well adjusted adults.

A critique of traditional forms of developmental psychology combined with an exposure of the mixed messages of child oriented policy goals has the potential to revolutionise our valuing of children and childhood, re-positioning the child, not as the adult they will become but as the person they are in the here and now. This means that we need to listen to children, to engage with them in more attentive ways which will help us deepen our understanding of their lives. The childhood revolution can be most simply characterised as a valuing of children's wellbeing in the present moment rather than an investment in their future psychological health and economic productiveness.

2
Life chances and longitudinal studies

What do I know of man's destiny? I could tell you more about radishes.
Samuel Beckett

Introduction

The children who have so generously contributed to this study have been engaged in it from the age of three until seventeen. It is unusual to find a longitudinal study in which the researcher has worked with their research participants over such a long time. This Chapter considers why longitudinal studies of a qualitative nature like this one remain so rare, discusses the few similar studies and recognises the enormously important contribution that such studies can make to theoretical understandings of the changes occurring over the lifespan and to policy on child wellbeing. It becomes clear that we need longitudinal studies such as this one in order to explore links between early experiences and later outcomes.

Within the discipline of child development there has been a strong assumption that what happens in early childhood, especially within significant family relationships, *determines* the life chances of children and sets up patterns for their future pathways through life. In the last chapter we saw that this assumption has resulted in policies for early years care and education that value the child in the future rather than at the present. The taken for granted nature of infant determinism has been exposed and challenged by critical child developmental theorists such as Greene (1999), Burman (2008) and Guldberg (2009). Burman, for example, suggests that a 'scientific demand for ... prediction' under-lies traditional approaches to developmental psychology (p5). Guld-berg exposes the infant determinism that is present in much popular psychology, for example Oliver James' book (2002) *They F*** You Up: How to Survive Family Life* and Sue Gerhardt's (2004) *Why Love Matters: How Affection Shapes a Baby's Brain*. Guldberg argues that infant deter-minism is a myth, challenging the idea that what happens within the first three years is decisive for later outcomes, as so many develop-mental psychologists and psychoanalysts have argued. We have to ground this debate in real life longitudinal studies in order to under-stand more about how, and why, some life events will exert lasting in-fluences whilst other apparently significant events won't. Similarly, we have to understand more about how some life events have a long lasting impact on some individuals but not others.

The long and the short of it: how long is a longitudinal study?

The study forming the basis for this book is a qualitative longitudinal study as opposed to a quantitative longitudinal study. Quantitative longitudinal studies of children's development over time are able to show large scale patterns of change based on very large data sets. Three such studies are currently ongoing: The *Millennium Cohort Study* tracks the lives of 19,000 children born in 2000/2001, whilst two earlier birth cohort studies were begun in 1970 (*British Cohort Study*) and 1958 (*National Child Development Study*). More information about these three studies and the broad findings they reveal can be gained from the Centre for Longitudinal Studies. The *Millennium Cohort Study* has re-cently produced a report of the children at the age of five and is able to show trends concerning diet, gender differences in learning develop-ment, patterns of family composition, family reading behaviour and punishments.

Mason (1996) defines qualitative research as 'interpretivist, based on methods of analysis that involve complexity, and recognises the impor-tance of the social context in which data is produced' (p4). In describing the main attributes of qualitative longitudinal research, Saldana (2003) identifies three key attributes, which are: duration, time, and change. He also says that 'longitudinal means a looooong time'. This is an interesting remark as others use the term 'longitudinal' to describe quite a range of study durations, some as short as two or three years (Holland *et al*, 2006). The present study has run over thirteen to fourteen years and in this respect is a 'loooong study'. But the data collection has been intermittent over this period, as I describe below.

The UK funding body, the Economic and Social Research Council (ESRC), has recently invested in re-use of archived qualitative data, for example the *Inventing Adulthoods* study with 100 young people over 10 years (Henderson *et al*, 2007) and has also commissioned the innovative Timescapes study (http://www.timescapes.leeds.ac.uk/), demonstrating new commitment to longitudinal qualitative research. An overview of the emerging genre of qualitative longitudinal research studies (QLR) has been undertaken by Holland *et al* (2006), who have become advocates for this methodology since a milestone conference at South Bank University in London in 2002 which drew together interdisciplinary studies. The common element was that 'temporality is designed into the research process making change a central focus of analytic attention' (Thomson *et al*, 2003:185).

Of most relevance is the *Identity Learning Programme* conducted by Pollard and Filer (Pollard, 2007), along with the *12-18 project* conducted in Melbourne, Australia from 1994-2001, funded by the Australian Research Council (Yates and McLeod, 1996; 2006). This followed young people from a range of backgrounds located in four different schools. It focused in particular on the impact of the school on their life pathways. Holland *et al* also discuss the research that was undertaken by Walkerdine *et al* (2001) and reported in their book *Growing Up Girl*. This draws on data from a twenty year period, following up the girls who originally formed a sample for the classic study by Tizard and Hughes into young children's language practices at home and school (1984). However, the work of these authors has not been a continuing ethnography of individual lives so much as an intermittent revisiting of the sample, using repeat interviews and video diaries and harnessed to a specific concern with social class. Their study has been particularly persuasive with regard to the recognition of emotional dimensions within the research relationship and this dimension is discussed in greater detail in Chapter 5.

The review by Holland *et al* presents three different categories of the QLR genre, allowing me to position my own study within it. These authors identify firstly, continuous research in the same small society over a number of years; secondly, periodic studies at regular or irregular intervals; and thirdly, studies in which the researchers return after a lengthy interval of time (p5). The study discussed in this book overlaps these categories, as now described.

When I began this study I had planned that it would be longitudinal in the sense that the period of data collection would occur over a three year period, from the year before the children started formal schooling though the first year of school (known as Reception class in the English school system), into the second year. This period constitutes a relatively short longitudinal study according to the above overview of QLR categories. The time-frame, selected in order to learn how children develop a sense of self during the transition into the social world of early school, was also influenced by the hidden constraints that are implicated in a funded full time PhD, as that is what the first phase of this study was. In their overview of qualitative longitudinal studies, Holland *et al* show that many short longitudinal studies exist and that is probably because funding bodies are only willing to commit to a maximum time phase of three years or so. In order to write up the study as a PhD thesis I needed to call a definite halt to the process of data collection, which I did when the children were well established in their primary schools. I wrote up the study and got my PhD. End of story. But of course it wasn't.

Curiosity is an unsung hero within qualitative longitudinal research. In my case it became an active driver of the study's continuation. I wanted, quite simply, to know what had happened to the children. Their stories were not finished and I had left the children at interesting points on their journeys into the further reaches of school. In the case of certain individuals there were some particularly tantalising cliffhangers. Would Shelley's school career be dogged by the strong disapproval she had experienced from her first teachers, who perceived her as antisocial? Would David's popularity with his group of very lively mates and simultaneous distancing from his teachers lead him to develop an anti-school peer culture? Would Liam be able to recover the academic ground he had lost because of the failure to recognise the extent of his deafness? What significant events might occur in the children's lives?

Would some parents split up? Would some re-partner? Would new brothers or sisters be born? Would there be a change of housing or a new school? I wanted to find out.

However, my own life story was unfolding at a fast and furious pace. I had a new and fascinating research study as a post doctoral researcher in a different university department and then moved into further lecturing jobs, away from the town in which I had conducted the study. My paid employment together with my unpaid employment as a parent meant that these questions went underground. It was seven years before I was able to find the time, the finances and the commitment necessary to pick up the fragments of these stories and re-enter them.

My plans to track the children seven years after I had last seen them were not only influenced by curiosity. I was also inspired by the few but significant examples of researchers who had followed up their samples in the way that I proposed. Most particularly I was influenced by the work of Pollard and Filer in the *Identity Learning Programme* (see Pollard, 2007). Their tracking of children through primary schooling and into secondary school was a major influence on my decision to follow up the children in my own study, particularly as they too had been interested in issues about identity, the concept of the individual's strategic biography, and the related idea of the pupil career. Rather more indirectly, the classic *7 Up* series suggested a model of follow-up, especially as, coincidentally, it had been a seven year gap between the first phase of the study and the second. This series of TV/film documentaries, initiated by Michael Apted, has followed the lives of fourteen British children since 1964 when they were aged seven, producing an update every seven years. The current TV series *Child of Our Time* (BBC) presented by Robert Winston has also been inspirational, as it is also a longitudinal study in which a sample of children are revisited over time. Following children born in 2000, it is about to embark on its tenth series. However, these last two sources of inspiration were produced specifically for the medium of TV and combined entertainment alongside research, and they do not specifically address the construction of self.

Inspired by the models of longitudinal research in which cases have been followed up over childhood and beyond, I decided to track down nine of the original ten children in the sample. The tenth child, Ghita, had moved to another part of England midway through the first phase of the study and although I had maintained contact with her by phone, I lost contact when she moved for a second time. I turned myself into a sleuth and began making contact with the nine children on the basis of the contact addresses and telephone numbers I had filed seven years previously. In some cases it was easy. Jayne, David, Simon and Umar had all remained in the same home. Anna was hard to track down. The family who had moved into her old home knew that Anna's mother worked as a hairdresser and I only located her through trial and error, searching the hairdressing salons in the town. In the cases of Martin and Liam, I had had fortuitous accidental meetings (with Martin's Mum and with Liam) in the intervening period in which I had opportunistically gained new contact details. In some cases the search was a tortuous process and I owe a debt of gratitude to the children's neighbours and the new occupiers of their old homes. In Chapter 4 I discuss the ethical and relational aspects of re-establishing contact with the children and their families and gaining consent to continue the study.

The nine children and their parents all gave consent for me to continue with the study, which meant visiting them in their homes on three different occasions during the course of their second year at secondary school (year 8 in the UK system). I was extremely grateful. I was also grateful to my institution for providing a small grant to enable the depth of follow up I planned during this year and that allowed me to engage a research assistant, Janine Muldoon. During this year I was able to make three sequential visits to the children, to talk with them and carry out a raft of strategies I'd devised for accessing their self beliefs. This was an opportune time for the children to look back on the transition from primary to secondary school and offer ideas about how this change in context had influenced the construction of self. After this intensive, funded phase of the study, my continuing contact was on a much more sporadic basis during the remainder of these young people's school career. A round of further interviews took place two years later, at the age of fifteen, again with an explicit focus on perceptions of identity and change. Finally I sought them out when they were seventeen and held a number of further conversations focused on their understandings of self, a retrospective view of changes during their years of schooling and discussion of their aspirations and anxieties for the future.

The value of qualitative longitudinal research is that it can be 'highly sensitive to contextual issues, and can illuminate important micro-social processes, such as the ways in which people subjectively negotiate the changes that occur in their lives at times of personal life transition' (Henwood and Lang, 2003:49). In particular, as now discussed, it is only through qualitative studies conducted over a long phase of the lifespan that we can start to understand answers to questions about the life chances of individuals, their responses to adversity and good fortune.

Fortune telling: life chances and resilience

Perhaps the success of the long established *Up* series for TV and the recent *Child of Our Time* is that these programmes provide the public with an opportunity for testing out their fortune telling abilities. Our enjoyment of making predictions is based, however, on a deeply embedded assumption about lifespan development. We believe that the experiences of early infancy cause particular human responses in later life, a belief that can be characterised as psychological determinism. One of the questions I want to open up through the stories in this book is how far we can anticipate future outcomes for an individual on the basis of insights into their younger lives.

The case studies presented in Chapters 6-9 show that the children's lives as adolescents and young adults could not be predicted on the basis of the observations I had made of them in their early life. Indeed my attempts at fortune telling were often way off the mark. You can perhaps imagine the feelings of anticipation and curiosity that dominated my first meeting with the children after a lapse of seven years. Would I be able to recognise them? How would they have changed? I made guesses, telling myself different stories about how they would have settled into secondary school, the quality of their peer relationships and the likeli-hood of academic success.

The greatest surprise was to find out that Kelley, the good little girl of my early study, had been excluded from two different schools by the time I met her again. Reflecting on my failure to predict this poor school out-come, I have come up with three related explanations. Firstly, I had given too much weight to her teachers' extremely positive judgments about her first years at school ('wonderful', 'mature and helpful') and not enough to her family circumstances. Secondly, my methods of data collection had not given me a full enough picture of her world to provide a reliable basis for predictions. These explanations suggest that my research methods and interpretations were inadequate. However, a third explanation would be to critique my over reliance on a simple casual link between the behaviours of early childhood and later developmental outcomes. Burman (2008) exposes the 'developmental fallacy that earlier behaviours must be causally related to subsequent developmental achievement' (p55).

The idea that the experiences of early childhood exert a crucial influence on adulthood is integral to psychoanalytic, Freudian influenced theories of development. It is also embedded in ideas about self fulfilling prophesies, for example based on the classic study by Rosenthal and Jacobsen (1968), suggesting that the expectations that are directed at the young child create the first step in a chain of expectation and con-sequent performance. It is a basic tenet of theories about early attach-ment relationships influenced by the work of Bowlby, claiming that the quality of infant attachments with parents has a lasting influence on a person's capacity for forming later attachments and relationships. We now take this idea for granted and, in particular, we believe that adverse events in childhood will scar a developing child for life. A number of famous cases of childhood deprivation have been used to support this view, especially cases of 'feral children' raised in social isolation and with non-existent or severely impaired parenting, such as Genie, who was locked in her bedroom until the age of thirteen (Curtiss, 1977). There has also been an increasing tide of claims about the extent to which early adverse experiences determine brain development. A belief has been built up that the positive psychosocial experiences in the first three years of life have a much greater impact and influence on the individual than similar experiences at a later stage because early experiences bring about a lasting change in brain structure (Gerhardt, 2004).

However, during the last two decades postmodernist thought has entered into and disturbed these traditional assumptions and some writers have begun to present critiques of traditional child psychology deconstructing some of its underpinnings and, in particular, exposing the 'myth of infant determinism' (Burman, 2008; Guldberg, 2008). Greene (1999) recognises awareness in contemporary thinking of 'the erratic and variable nature of psychological change and the extent to which change is a product of exchanges with the external environment rather than a matter of the unfolding of inherent potential' (p25), as suggested by developmentalists such as Piaget and Kohlberg. Barrett (2006) exposes the underlying determinism inherent in attachment theory in a measured presentation of the debate between determinists and constructivists. She concludes that, on balance, 'the human psyche, like human bones, is strongly inclined towards self healing', a quotation she provocatively lifts from Bowlby (1988:152), who is generally portrayed as the proponent of the irreparable nature of poor early attachment. Tizard (1991) argues that theories of the permanent effects of early experiences are too simplistic. She evidences cases that show that reversibility of fortunes can occur, for example the dramatic case of the Czech twins who made a remarkable recovery from the severe adverse experiences of their early childhood, and Moskovitz's (1985) study of survivors from a German concentration camp (p69). Tizard also claims that a secure early childhood is not necessarily an insurance against later psychological damage.

Rutter's work has made a significant contribution to the mounting critique of infant determinism and has foregrounded the concept of resilience. He studied a sample of children who had all suffered similar kinds of deprivation, as all had been brought up in appalling conditions in Romanian orphanages. These children, discovered at the end of Ceausescu's regime in 1989 and then adopted into UK families, showed a remarkable level of catch-up with regard to their cognitive development. Rutter portrays these cases as a striking example of what is meant by resilience, a concept that he defines as 'relatively good psychological functioning despite the experience of serious psychosocial adversities' (2002:8). This, he reminds us, is not a fixed human quality, and he is critical of claims, such as those made by Gerhardt (2004), that early experiences shape the brain in ways that remain permanent. He recognises that the variation of catch-up means it is impossible to understand precisely what mechanisms are responsible and he points to a vast array of different, interacting features in people's responses to risks and adversity. These include the history of the individual with respect to previous responses, their psychic make-up, their handling of the stress at the time, and their subsequent chain of responses. An interesting question arises about the extent to which an adverse event makes a person more resistant or more vulnerable to later psychosocial threats, a question that is relevant in the five following stories.

Is it a stroke of good fortune that some children just seem to be born with a more resilient and optimistic outlook than others? Or is this a quality that educators and parents could actively encourage and maintain? Several social and educational interventional programmes have been designed to try to instill the quality of resilience. For example 'Bounce Back' was devised in Australia (2006) by two educational psychologists, Noble and McGrath, and has now been taken up in schools in Scotland. Researchers have begun to identify good family relationships as a key component of resilience and a buffer against adversity. For example Iacovou (2004) cites Bergman and Scott (2001), who drew on the British Household Panel Survey data to find that good communication with parents makes it less likely that young people will be involved in risky behaviour. If we can analyse the components of resilience, and if we can work out how to promote it, and preserve it, then educators and carers of children will be on the way to improving children's wellbeing.

Conclusion

It is important for research to open up assumptions about the long term impact of early childhood disadvantage and its determining impact on later outcomes. Qualitative longitudinal research, still at an emergent stage as a new methodology, has the potential to help us do this. It can remind us to be suspicious of simplistic casual links between childhood and adulthood experiences, recognising that the only thing that is predictable is unpredictability. We can learn from cases where resilience has been in evidence and children have demonstrated that the human individual is capable of picking themselves up, dusting themselves down and starting all over again (to quote Nat King Cole's lyrics). One key component of resilience may be the ability to make and remake self. The capacity to tell a story of self and to change this narrative provides a strategy for coping with the slings and arrows of outrageous fortune. The next chapter explores this further.

3

Telling stories: the making and re-making of selves

As human beings our greatness lies not so much in being able to remake the world ... as in being able to remake ourselves. Gandhi

Introduction: why study the 'self'?

When we construct a self we are simultaneously creating the lenses through which we see the world and forming the bedrock of our mental health and wellbeing. Our ability to be reflexive, that is to be aware of our selves, to watch and evaluate our own behaviour, seems to be an ability that is profoundly human. Jerome Bruner, the famous psychologist of education who sought to describe what is uniquely individual about human beings, said that 'the phenomenon of self is perhaps the single most universal thing about human experience' (1996:35). If this is so then we need to understand much more about how we create self, why and when we do so. These questions, though they may seem rather abstract, have a direct bearing on the realities of teaching children and developing educational policy. Indeed, 'the theorisation of identity is a matter of considerable political significance' (Hall and du Gay, 1996:17).

Self, or identity, is interlinked with psychological health and wellbeing. Erikson, who studied human development across the lifespan, claimed that 'an increasing sense of identity ... is expressed as a sense of psycho-social wellbeing' (1980:127). His linking of identity with overall mental health sums up the views of many key thinkers in the related disciplines of psychology, sociology, philosophy and education (Mead, 1934; Maslow, 1954; Laing, 1960; Rogers, 1961, 1983; Giddens, 1991). Seligman's recent popular work on positive psychology reinforces a value for self-knowledge through the awareness of personal strengths as a route to mental health (Seligman, 2002). Many academics and policy-makers, from government ministers to school heads, are currently drawn to this approach, including the economist Layard, who supports Seligman's ideas in his discussion of 'happiness' (2005) and has also applied them in his consideration of values for improving childhood (Layard and Dunn, 2009). Identity is of considerable interest to politicians since it is such a fundamental part of wellbeing.

Wellbeing has become the focus of many policy domains such as health, education, housing, and employment. Perhaps the rather bland nature of the term means that it can operate as an umbrella concept for drawing together different policy areas. Consequently it lends itself well to the 'joined-up thinking' approach beloved by the Labour government, who have made frequent use of the term in recent years, for example in commissioning the Foresight (science and technology) project on Mental Capital and Wellbeing (2006-2008). The term has become a particular focus of policy-making for children and young people (Coleman, 2009).

A report by the Economic and Social Research Council (ESRC) began with the claim: 'How to secure our children's wellbeing is the question currently energising society as whole' (Bradshaw *et al*, 2007:2). This presented an overview of recent policy initiatives on wellbeing for children, based on a multi-dimensional interpretation of wellbeing that included wealth, health, educational achievement, family relationships, and safe environments. The much publicised UNICEF report (2007) on child poverty across 21 rich (OECD) countries prompted a burst of policy energy focused on child wellbeing. This report claimed to be a comprehensive assessment of the lives and wellbeing of children and adolescents in the economically advanced nations (see Chapter 1 for further discussion). The UNICEF findings about one particular indicator, children's subjective wellbeing, were especially relevant to debates about the nature and function of identity. Children in the UK scored badly and were placed at the bottom of the subjective wellbeing table.

Coleman (2009) points out the large number of policy initiatives from the UK government that have identified ways that schools can promote wellbeing. He cites a number of key influences on this political focus, including the UNICEF report. He also mentions the popularity of Goleman's ideas about emotional intelligence, and recent findings about high levels of mental health problems in children and young people in the UK (10% according to Melzer *et al*, 2000, cited by Coleman, 2009). Politicians and educators aiming to improve child wellbeing need to enter debates about the development of identity during childhood and adolescence, since social and emotional aspects of wellbeing are linked to the need for a clear sense of self. The final section of this book addresses recommendations for policy-makers and practitioners within education.

That self awareness and closely related concepts have value has become firmly established in educational policy in the UK. For example the *Birth to Three Matters Framework* (Sure Start, 2005) recommends the development of 'the strong self' as a key goal incorporating four elements: 'me, myself and I'; 'being acknowledged and affirmed'; 'developing self-assurance' and 'a sense of belonging'. Underlying this prescription is an assumption that an ability to know ourselves is an essential tool for life. *Excellence and Enjoyment*, the Government's strategy for primary schools (DfES, 2003) also presents primary education as a key opportunity for 'developing self-confidence as learners' as well as 'maturing socially and emotionally' (p1). The UK's SEAL programme (social and emotional aspects of learning), first piloted in a sample of primary schools 2003-2005, involves the use of curriculum materials as well as 'whole school' strategies to develop children's social and emotional abilities within five themes: self-awareness, managing feelings, motivation, empathy, and social skills. The materials include a unit entitled *Good to be me*.

The year 2009 saw the publication of two reviews of primary education: the Rose Report (Rose, 2009) commissioned by the government and the Cambridge Primary Review, an independent and altogether more radical review of primary education, chaired by Robin Alexander (2010). The Rose Report recommends six 'areas of learning', one of which is 'Understanding physical development, health and wellbeing', and which is intended to incorporate the existing SEAL programme. In the

31

Cambridge Review of Primary Education there is a more specific focus on the construction of self. This is incorporated into two of the twelve recommended aims: the promotion of a 'strong sense of self' (within the 'wellbeing' aim) and the promotion of 'respect for self' (within the broader 'encouraging respect and reciprocity' aim).

Secondary schools in the UK have given far less curriculum space to social and emotional aspects of learning since their curriculum has been driven by a standards agenda, even more than in primary schooling. But the Secondary SEAL pilot programme was rolled out to secondary schools in 2005. Given the new found emphasis on identity issues within these policies, such as strength of self, it is important to tease out underlying assumptions about what self is and why it matters.

Identity is not only an underpinning of wellbeing, it is also the lens through which we see and interpret the world around us. Our beliefs about self operate to select, filter and organise our perceptions of everything we encounter, and influence our making of meaning. Aspects of self which have greater significance for us operate as a stronger filter of experience than less significant aspects, influencing the way we extract self-relevant information and exclude self-irrelevant information. So the concept of identity has the explanatory power to reveal the underlying process of learning, why and how we learn. Researching the construction of identity is therefore a vitally important enterprise for anybody interested in processes of learning and teaching.

Do we need a 'self'? The chameleon and the snail

Several poststructuralist academics and researchers have recently begun to tease apart the concept of identity, suggesting that it is an illusory concept (Walkerdine, 1981; Hollway, 1989; Davies and Harre, 1990; Gergen, 1991; Kearney, 2003). This idea rests on the recognition that a person inhabits many social contexts throughout their lives and their sense of self is created through the range of social interactions in which they participate. So a person's sense of self varies according to each particular social context they find themselves in.

Imagine, for example, the typical morning spent by fourteen year old Anna (one of the nine children in the study, whose story is not told in this book). She gets up, spends some time interacting with her mother, has a quick breakfast whilst talking with her stepfather and mother, catches the school bus, which is populated with a mix of familiar and unfamiliar fellow pupils, pops into the newsagents near school to buy a snack, where she talks briefly with the salesperson, enters her class-room and speaks with her form tutor about an absence note, takes part in a school assembly, chats in the corridor with her two best friends, goes to her first lesson in which pupils are set according to ability, and then meets her own group of friends in the playground at break-time. Concerns about her identity are probably the last thing on Anna's mind as she experiences this sequence of social encounters. They are unlikely to be activated unless, let us imagine, the salesperson, her mother's friend, remarks that she is looking tired, or perhaps her friend requests help with homework because Anna is 'really good at History'. At such moments, issues about identity will come to the fore as Anna tries to interpret these comments, confronting another person's perception of her. An individual's understanding about who they are, at any moment in time, is influenced by the ways they see themselves within a parti-cular social group and by the ways the others in the group see them. Anna's experience of many different social groups makes for a multiple sense of self.

Taken to its logical conclusion, this perspective suggests that we may not be able to contain the lived range of multiple selves within the straight-jacketing concept of 'self'. That is why many authors who em-phasise the ever-changing nature of self prefer to exchange the term 'identity' for 'identities' (see poststructuralist theorists listed above). This approach draws attention to the dynamism of co-existing and competing selves and minimises the unifying aspects of self. It invites us to imagine to what extent we could do without identity. Engaging in this 'thought experiment' leads us to ask what purpose identity serves. One answer, as we have seen, is that the self is an untenable concept which simply cannot capture the complexities and inconsistencies of real lives. This is a very different answer to the view that is taken for granted in the wellbeing policies presented above where a 'strong sense of self' is assumed to be the basis for mental health and psychological wellbeing.

These two answers are the products of diametrically opposed theories of self. The first stresses the changeability of self: identity does not exist outside of the social context in which it is constructed. It is like a chameleon that changes its colour according to its environment. The second approach stresses the continuity of self: something that the person carries about with them through time and through the range of social situations they participate in. It is like a snail's shell, carried about by the snail wherever it goes. This fanciful contrast highlights the need to recognise the implicit theories that underlie policies. So it is useful to draw out some further differences in identity theories that educational policy makers and practitioners need to be aware of.

Theoretical tensions

The social psychologist Asch (1952:251), who studied group processes, insisted that we need to understand the reality of 'individual *and* group', and he described these as 'the two permanent poles of all social processes'. Sociologist Giddens (1984) similarly saw the need to reconcile the individual actor (agency) and the social structures that exist around them (structure). In planning and implementing the longitudinal study presented in this book and analysing the data it produced I have tried to maintain this interwoven connection by keeping a perspective on the individual and simultaneously on their social context. I start by declaring that the self is essentially a social concept. This can seem a rather paradoxical claim so let me explain.

This starting point has been influenced by two key thinkers. The first is the Russian psychologist Lev Vygotsky whose theories about the nature of thought and learning were translated into English and widely disseminated, especially in the world of initial teacher training, during the eighties and nineties. Vygotsky emphasised the social origins of thought:

> All the higher order mental functions are interiorised relations of a social order, the basis of the social structure of the personality ... all of their nature is social: even when alone man retains the functions of communication. (1991:41)

An individual's mental construction of their personal identity is produced through social contact. It is not innate within the infant but arises through the first social relationships.

My second key thinker is George Herbert Mead, whose discussion of the links between mind, self and society in his classic book of that name (1934) began, like Vygotsy, with acknowledgement of the self as a social product. He believed that the individual develops an internal representation of the self through social interaction:

> The self is something which has a development; it is not initially there at birth, but arises in the process of social experience and activity...The self, as that which can be an object to itself, is essentially a social structure. (1934:135)

Both Mead and Vygotsky emphasise the two way direction of influence between the individual and their social environment. The link between these two thinkers has been observed by writers interested in identity (for example Davies, 1987; Woodhead and Light, 1991; Pollard and Filer, 1996; Kearney, 2003). We are only capable of constructing a self when we are able to interpret the response our behaviour evokes in others and to use this understanding to control our own further conduct. Awareness of self and evaluations of self develop interdependently with awareness and evaluations of others.

Alongside growing recognition during the last half of the twentieth century of the socially situated nature of self, theoretical approaches to identity were strongly influenced by the 'psy specialists', the term adopted by Rose (1997) to represent the whole gamut of identity experts, such as psychologists, counsellors, therapists, and self help gurus. They believed that identity is located within the individual and is waiting to be discovered or liberated from repression. For example, humanistic psychologists Maslow and Rogers promoted this view with their emphasis on 'self actualisation' (Maslow, 1954) and the search for the person that one 'truly' is (Rogers, 1961, 1983). Traditional psychological measures of self concept, such as Marsh's Self Description Questionnaire (1992), pre-suppose that fully formed self-beliefs reside in the mind of an individual and are available to the interested researcher, teacher or psychologist who can lure them out. These theories emphasise several inter-related attributes of the self: it is individual, continuous across time, coherent across social contexts, and unified into a consistent whole.

This idea of self has been challenged from several quarters for a number of reasons. As we have seen, poststructuralist theorists have drawn attention to the multiplicity of selves, suggesting there is no continuous self that can be carried from one social situation to another because the self does not exist outside the social relationships within which it is created. The idea of the continuous consistent self has also been challenged by those who see this kind of self construction as individualist. Feminist writers (Grimshaw, 1986; Miller, 1988) have shown that this approach does not take account of the interdependent relationships between people. For a parent with dependent children, for example, the nurturing of self is interwoven with the nurturing of others. Writers have criticised the individualism underlying modern western society and the emphasis on self within this culture (Hargreaves, 1982; Bauman, 2001; Beck and Beck-Gernsheim, 2002; Ecclestone and Hayes, 2008; Craig, 2009). In their recent inquiry into the quality of modern childhood, Layard and Dunn (2009) suggest that 'excessive individualism' is a common theme linking the various problems of childhood in the UK. These related critiques, from anti-individualist, feminist and post-structuralist researchers, challenge traditional psychological constructions of identity as pre-given, unitary, consistent and individualistic.

This is an appropriate point at which to say more about the problematic concept of self esteem (which takes centre stage in Jayne's story, Chapter 8), since it relates to individualism. This is an extremely prevalent concept within educational discourse and is used as a cure-all for a whole range of childhood and educational problems (Kahne, 1996; Emler, 2001; Baumeister *et al*, 2003; Craig, 2009). Secondly, it is a very vague concept. There has been a vast literature debating what exactly self esteem is, whether it represents a general or domain specific aspect of self, and how it can be measured (Byrne, 1996; Hattie, 1992). Emler's overview of the literature (2001) concludes that there is not yet any agreement amongst academics about its nature or measurement. It is perhaps precisely because it is a rather vague term that it is so widely used, a point made by Kahne (1996) who identifies it as a manipulative concept.

Thirdly, and my reason for mentioning it in relation to the above comments about individualism, self esteem elevates the individualistic aspects of self formation and under-emphasises the social. Emler suggests that over-inflated self esteem maybe as much a social problem as low self esteem. Young-Eisandrath (2009) claims that Western parents are trapped by the desire to raise exceptional children who are high in self esteem. Craig (2009) is critical of the American 'self esteem movement', believing that the emphasis on raising self esteem can lead to valuing self obsession and arrogance. Within the world of educational policy-making we attach too much importance to self esteem. We have not managed to maintain a balance between an emphasis on the individual and the group, as identified by Asch. Our emphasis has slipped too far to the individualist pole.

Telling stories of self: the desire and capacity for narrative

In emphasising the socially situated nature of self as I have done here, I have not yet mentioned the role of time. Yet identity is continuous over time, 'life-long' as well as 'life-wide'. It is important to look at how self construction occurs over time, as this concerns a person's capacity to change, to learn or fail to learn, to be open or resistant to new influences. A belief about self that becomes entrenched over time (for example 'I am not a mathematician') then operates as a lens or set of blinkers (Kelly, 1955) filtering out self- irrelevant aspects of the environment (numbers). Carol Dweck (2000) argues that the reason so many people hold fixed, 'entity' theories of self is that it provides them with a sense of security, a feeling that they know themselves and they know the others around them. She suggests, however, that over rigid, entrenched beliefs about self stand in the way of change and adaptability: we need to be able to remake ourselves, to have 'incremental selves' that can be expanded and flexible. We have a strong motivation to create a pattern or form to our self beliefs as they emerge over time. Swann's work draws attention to this desire to create a coherent or consistent self, to 'self-verify' (Swann *et al*, 1989; Swann, 1990). It is necessary to find ways of representing the self that shows it is flexible, that it can be made and remade, but that it has continuity over time. The concept of narrative or story can help us here.

The metaphor of 'story' provides a way of resolving the theoretical tensions identified above. A story (history, biography) can hold fragments together (plots and sub plots) and create form but it can be flexible and can be remade when necessary. The construction of self can be viewed as the creation of narrative, a sense-making device, which provides the appearance of a pattern through repetition of characteristics over time. We 'hear and understand in narratives' (Gud-mundsdottir 1996:291 cited in Sumison, 1999:456), imposing a narrative structure on our experiences as a way of managing them. Giddens (1991) has chosen this metaphor to present identity, defining it as 'an ongoing 'story' about the self' (p54). Other sociological and social psychological theorists have also recognised the value of describing the construction of self as story making (Dennet, 1991; Benhabib, 1992; Griffiths, 1995; Rose, 1997; Munro, 1998; Kearney, 2003; Hall and du Gay, 2006). Story making is an appropriate metaphor for the construction of self for yet another reason, that relates back to the discussion above. It is an essentially social, rather than individual activity. The drive to tell a story of self is socially motivated, a form of communication between teller and told, and is different for different audiences.

Portraying identity in this way emphasises its language demands. The recent and popular idea of 'emotional literacy' (Weare, 2004) suggests the need for children to develop emotional vocabulary. Exposure to and practice in the use of emotional vocabulary seems an essential requirement in advocating the value of stories of self. Emotional literacy is not just about vocabulary but can also encompass the narrative skills of weaving together the different threads of a story of self – what Giddens terms 'capacity to keep a particular narrative going'.

The terms 'emotional literacy' and 'emotional intelligence' are now common in the talk of teachers and educational policy makers. Coleman (2009) cites the influential work of Daniel Goleman (1996) on emotional intelligence as one of the key drivers of the current policy emphasis on children's psychological and emotional wellbeing. Although many are sceptical about the validity of some of Goleman's arguments, as Coleman points out, there is little doubt that his book *Emotional Intelligence* has acted as a magnet for attracting public interest in emotional health. More recently (2007) Goleman has advocated 'social intelligence', to emphasise the capacity to manage well within a group, a switch that indicates a shift from the interpersonal to the intrapersonal. The term 'relational intelligence', or 'relational awareness', might provide an effective alternative, operating to draw together these intelligences. 'Relational' emphasises human relationships between people and as such it seems the most accurate term to capture the interplay between the individual and the social, expressing both at once. Creating stories of self occurs in interaction with others. It is a practice which clearly entails all kinds of 'intelligence': 'emotional' and 'social'. But it is fundamentally a relational practice with a relational outcome. (I use the terms 'relational intelligence' and 'relational aware-ness' interchangeably).

Conclusion: the social nature of self and the capacity for narrating self stories

The self is social and it is changeable. Our energies as teachers and carers of the next generation should be focused on facilitating a capa-city for telling a story of self rather than creating a strong sense of self. This is a subtle but important difference. It emphasises adaptability and the chameleon-like nature of the self as it changes according to the social context. However it also suggests a value for the ability to inte-grate different selves into a coherent and continuing narrative.

The next Chapter expands on the idea that self understanding is built up alongside and as part of social understanding. It begins by exploring the origins of this dual process in early childhood and then considers the impact of the social organisation of childhood and adolescence, namely schooling.

4

Narrating self through childhood
and beyond

Freud, writing on the child's self-love and the later development of the ability to love others, said that 'his egoism has taught him to love' (1966, p.204). What I propose here is that the child's egoism in the context of family relationships motivates him to understand others. Dunn, 1988:82

The beginnings of relational awareness

We now turn our attention to the distinctiveness of childhood and adolescence as a context for the ongoing creation of self. We look at the developmental capacities of young children and adolescents in constructing their identities and reflect on children's social groups, particularly in the mini society of school. Let us start with the developmental theorists whose ideas seem most useful when trying to understand the stories of self created by Martin, Shelley, Simon, Jayne and Liam.

There are many accounts of the construction of self in childhood and adolescence, mostly based on psychological developmental research. These are often concerned with ages and stages of manifestations of specific self making abilities. Many are derived from Piaget's work on children's capacity to take on the perspectives of others (see Harter, 1999, for a good overview). Accounts of self construction start with the ability to recognise the self in a mirror, and then move on to the ability to recognise the self in the metaphorical mirror of other people's perceptions. The 'red spot' method, in which the infant has rouge dabbed on their nose in front of a mirror is the usual strategy for researching the young child's ability to self recognise. If the child touches their own nose rather than the mirror then self recognition is inferred. This usually occurs at between fifteen and twenty four months old (Lewis and Brooks-Gunn, 1979).

The next landmark stage, though altogether less discernible, is the capacity to understand the perspectives of another. This is a crucial development since it marks the change from the 'I' self to the 'me' self. This distinction was originally pointed out by William James (1890) who described the primitive 'I' self as knower, compared with the more advanced 'me' self, as known and objectified. Mead's words quoted in the last Chapter describe the 'me' self as 'that which can be an object to itself', drawing attention to the human capacity for reflexivity. Children develop a 'me' self through recognising that other people have minds and that they are forming opinions and perceptions of them. Cooley (1902) described this capacity as the 'looking glass self'.

There is a vast psychological literature on children's ability to recognise the perspectives of others. Much of this was prompted by Piaget's experiments on perspective taking and much of it is restricted to children's cognitive abilities to see what others see, a capacity described in the psychological developmental literature as children's 'theory of mind': the understanding that other people have minds (Baron-Cohen, 1991). Donaldson's contribution to this debate (1978) was to include emotional and social aspects of perspective taking and to show that when experiments made 'human sense' to children they demonstrated greater perspective taking abilities at younger ages than Piaget had found. A classic naturalistic study by Tizard and Hughes (1984) based in the home and not the laboratory also contained examples of very young children's abilities to understand the perspectives of others. For example these authors quote an extract from their tape recordings of conversations between mothers and four year old daughters, in which a four year old understands how she appears to her mother whilst she is upside down having her bottom wiped. This interaction and its demonstration of perspective taking abilities would not have been captured in a laboratory!

Child: Mummy you lost me.

Mother: I have lost you, yeah.

Child: Can you only see my bottom and legs?

Mother: That's right.

Child: And shoes and pants.

Mother: That's right.

Child: Here I am.

Mother: That's nice. There she is. Back again.

Judy Dunn's landmark study of young children's development of social understanding (1988) is relevant to discussion of the beginnings of relational awareness. Her study, too, was based in children's homes, where she observed young children interacting with siblings and with parents. In this naturalistic environment, that incorporates the 'emotionally urgent situations that occur within the family' (p180), she found evidence of an ability to understand the feeling states of others present in children as young as two years old. Her research shows how awareness of self and awareness of others develop simultaneously, and how a developing capacity in one area feeds a developing capacity in the other.

With regard to the development of self in adolescence, Erikson is particularly well known for his approach to this phase of life as the time for resolving identity crises and building up an integrated self. As part of his overall theory of psychosocial stages across the lifespan, Erikson (1980) sees the main task of adolescence as one of drawing together different aspects of self. Harter (1999) has provided an extremely detailed developmental account of the construction of self. Her portrayal of self construction during adolescence maps onto Erikson's in so far as it presents a motivation to make sense of competing selves. She presents the reflections of adolescents who recognise that they seem to be different people in different social groupings, experiencing a kind of 'identity dissonance' (Warin *et al*, 2006; Warin and Dempster, 2007) as they struggle to present a coherent account of self. Both writers recognise the urge for integration of selves in adolescence, supporting my emphasis on narrative as a means of fulfilling the desire to create a coherent account of self.

Group processes and school groups

The claim made above that identity is experienced and constructed through the experience of participating within society, within a social group, warrants further consideration. There are three key ways in which this is so. Firstly, interaction with others provides an individual with judgments and perspectives of their behaviour reflected back to them, the 'looking glass self'. Some judgments will be quite explicitly offered, for example a compliment from a teacher in a school report or an abusive statement from a bullying peer. Others may be rather more subtle. Feedback is then taken on board and used to create a 'me' self.

Secondly, a social group provides a 'reference group', the social psychological term used to indicate the group that an individual has in mind when they make social comparisons (Festinger, 1954). Social psychologists Tajfel and Turner (1979) have described how group formation and the construction of self are interdependent processes. Their work emphasises the forming of 'ingroups' and 'outgroups' as we associate with those who are 'like me', and dissociate from those who are 'unlike me'. Sociologists are likely to use the term 'othering' to describe the same process. For example Hey (1997) uses this term to describe the processes of group and subgroup formation in her study of the friendships and affiliations of secondary school girls. This basic human process of social inclusion with others who are perceived to be similar and social exclusion from those who are perceived to be dissimilar is essential to the construction of self, with group formation occurring at the same time as the formation of identity.

The third way that participation within a social group influences the construction of a self is that it creates occasions for the activation of self, the communication of the story of self. For example in my summary account of Anna's participation in a number of groups during a typical school morning, it was only those moments when she received comments from others (about her tired appearance and ability in History) that her reflection on self was activated.

Schools are mini societies comprised of a huge range of types of groups. As the ethnographer of schools Philip Jackson has pointed out 'Learning to live in classroom is like learning to live in a crowd' (Jackson, 1968:10). He draws attention to the ratio of many children to a small

44

number of adults as a significant aspect of classroom social dynamics. The complexities of classroom dynamics include relationships between peers, (pupil/pupil), relationships between teacher(s) and pupils (teacher/pupil) and more complex relationships as pupil/pupil inter-actions are influenced by teachers, and teachers are influenced by pupil/pupil interactions (teacher/pupil/pupil). This taken for granted aspect of classroom life is one reason that many children find it difficult to adapt to the formal schooling environment where they have to share adult attention, a feature of the initial transition into school that is clearly reflected in the following five stories.

Schools provide a range of social groups within which the individual pupil participates. There are formal groups prompted by the school as an organisation, such as school classes, year groups, sets, and allocation of pupils to work tables. There are informal groups in the form of friend-ship groups and wider sub-cultural groups, as children form their own associations with those they perceive to be similar, and dissociations from those they perceive to be dissimilar. These formal and informal groups become reference groups. Pollard (1987) provides an illustration in his ethnographic study of a top primary classroom, where he identi-fies the children's own sub groups: the goodies, jokers and gangs. Pollard (2008) shows how formal grouping, through school policies and teachers' classroom management, can challenge or reinforce peer net-works, and draws attention to how the resulting ingroups and out-groups become entrenched as children affirm their own sets of values and cultures. Building on the classic sociological studies of secondary schooling by Hargreaves (1967) and Lacey (1970), Pollard shows how the interaction of formal and informal school groups leads to a form of 'polarisation' as anti-school and pro-school attitudes are gradually developed. As opposite labels, these terms may appear to be rather simple yet they represent a process of entrenchment that occurs over time and through group formation that is anything but simple, can be-come very resistant to change, and significantly influences educational outcomes.

The impetus for telling stories of self. Transitions and fateful moments

A 'school career', the term used by Pollard and Filer to denote pathways through the formal years of school (1996, 1999), incorporates various transitional phases. In the UK these include the initial transition into formal compulsory schooling at age four/five, the significant change from primary schooling to secondary schooling, a further transition for some into further education or higher education and, for all, a move from educational institutions into the wider world. These educational transitions are significant phases within the construction of identity. They activate a story of self. When a person moves into an unfamiliar environment there is a volume of stimuli to make sense of, to absorb and to categorise. This creates cognitive pressure alongside emotional pressure since such phases are often characterised by feelings of anxiety about the unknown. Identity becomes a mechanism for coping. At such times a person may fall back on the more entrenched aspects of self such as gender which provide a tried and tested lens for filtering new information. (Jackson and Warin, 2000; Warin and Dempster, 2007). The transition also provides a new reference group, so there is an added impetus to the making of social comparisons.

Giddens (1991) links transitional phases across the lifespan with his focus on 'fateful moments' as prompts for re-appraising identity. Fateful moments create an interruption in the routine aspects of life, and during such moments 'no matter how reflexive an individual may be in the shaping of her self-identity, she has to sit up and take notice of new demands as well as new possibilities' (p142). When life has to be seen 'anew', says Giddens, there is an intensification of reflection about self, a crisis point in the ongoing story of self. The concept of 'fateful moments' has proved attractive to those concerned with significant emotional thresholds in the lives of children and young people. Denscombe (2000) harnesses this idea to elucidate the stressful nature of GCSEs. Henderson *et al* (2007) elaborated Giddens' concept in their study about the 'critical moments' experienced by young people inventing adulthoods as they move out of school. In the forthcoming stories I refer to the significance of each of the three key transitional phases of schooling as a cue for telling a story of self: school start, primary/ secondary transfer, and school exit.

The capacity for telling a story of self is an important tool for living, for coping with difficult and uncertain phases of life. Given its importance, we need to ask how it can be nurtured and whether it is equally available to everybody. Giddens' emphasis on the centrality of 'the reflexive project of the self' has been criticised, as it seems to imply that everybody is equally free and equally able to engage in this kind of self building activity (Rose, 1997; Skeggs, 2004; Henderson *et al*, 2007). This observation leads into the next point: the constraints that can inhibit a telling of self.

Does everybody have the capacity to create a story of self? Identity capital and inequalities

Drawing on the theories of Bourdieu, Coté (1996) used the term 'identity capital' to represent the idea that identity may be a form of social advantage. Sociologists influenced by the work of Bourdieu have adopted the term 'capital' to describe the stock of resources available to an individual or groups. Originally used to describe economic wealth, Bourdieu expanded the concept of capital to include cultural capital (Bourdieu and Passeron, 1977), which recognises that dominant groups (the powerful classes) are able to give status to their own cultural values (see Henderson *et al*, 2007 for an overview, and see Reay, 2004 for an expansion of 'cultural capital' to 'emotional capital'). Coté described identity capital as the extent to which a person 'invests in who they are' (Coté, 1996:425). He is interested in how social class influences this kind of investment. He acknowledges that a higher social class background bestows advantages in acquiring identity capital (p426), supporting the notion that the capacity to tell a story of self may be an activity or technique that is not available to everyone.

In the last Chapter I suggested that the capacity to tell a story of self relies on practice in emotional vocabulary and narrative skill. However, not all children have opportunities for the kind of abstract talk that produces a stock of rehearsed insights into self. Theorists interested in the relationships between language and social class (for example Barnes, 1976 based on earlier influential work by Bernstein, 1971) would support this argument. If identity capital is influenced by social class, education has a vital political role to play in ensuring that all children have access to language opportunities that allow them to invest in who they are, thereby creating this form of capital.

Conclusion

In this Chapter I emphasised the development of identity through early childhood as an interdependent growth of self awareness and awareness of others. By adolescence many have come to recognise the co-existence of competing selves, or dissonant identities. Theorists of this phase of the lifespan have pointed out an urge for the integration of selves, supporting the idea that narrative provides a way of making sense of experiences of different selves in different contexts. The capacity to tell a story of self is derived from social relationships whilst also facilitating the formation and progression of social relationships. Through childhood and adolescence the organisation of schooling creates the social context for the formation of ingroups and outgroups. Groups, formal and informal, are created on the basis of beliefs about peers who are 'like me' and peers who are 'unlike me'. So group formation occurs simultaneously with identity formation. School transitions operate as fateful moments within the construction of self as they activate self reflection, creating both the need and the opportunity for identity narratives.

The capacity to create an identity, described here as the capacity to tell a story of self, provides a form of social advantage or identity capital. Theorising about identity in this way has important repercussions on education policy and influences both curriculum and pedagogy. Education has the potential to bring about the opportunities and provide the resources that could enable *all* children to tell a story of self, ironing out disparities in this form of capital. Discussing the value of activities relating to identity construction leads to deeper questions about educational aims which in turn leads to deeper questions about the sort of society we want. These are questions that are reconsidered in the final section of this book, following the stories of Martin, Shelley, Simon, Jayne and Liam. It is to these five individuals that we now turn. In the next Chapter, I describe how the study was undertaken, and the strategies I adopted to understand these young people's processes of identity construction.

5

Creating a research relationship with children over a 14 year period

*The story-of-a-life as told to a particular person is in some sense a joint pro-
duct of the teller and the told. Selves, whatever metaphysical stand one takes
about the 'reality' can only be revealed in a transaction between a teller and
a told, ...whatever topic one approaches by interviewing must be evaluated
in the light of that transaction.* Bruner, J. 1990:124

The relational nature of research

All that has been revealed through research is a product of the human relationships in which the research has been embedded. Yet accounts of the research process are usually sanitised, omitting the messy and human aspects. The key point in this Chapter is that when we come to recognise that all research is relational, and when we start to look at how the socio-emotional aspects of the research relationship influence the collection and interpretation of data, the topic of research methods, which can sometimes seem a little dry, becomes much more human and humane. I will be exploring this point further as I reflect on the changing nature of my relationship with the children, their parents and teachers, providing an insight into methodological and ethical concerns particular to qualitative longitudinal research with children and young people.

My own methodological process is essentially about managing and developing sets of relationships, echoing the words of Bruner, above, which portray the data collection methods I have used as a co-construction. This approach matches the conclusion presented at the end of the previous Chapter: that the construction of identity is produced through the social relationship between teller and told.

In the introduction to this book I characterised this study as 'intermittent ethnography'. I now explain what I mean and describe some of the techniques and strategies I used with the children over the years to prompt their perceptions about their identity and the ways they had changed.

Ethnographers aim to understand their chosen setting from the *inside*. The ethnographer 'enters into a social setting and ... participates in the daily routines of this setting, develops ongoing relations with the people in it, and observes all the while what is going on' (Emerson, Fretz and Shaw, 1995:1). This definition draws out the traditional emphasis in ethnography on observation as well as the importance of understanding how those in the chosen field of study 'make sense of their world' (Wolcott, 1999:213; see also Pollard and Filer, 1999; Hamersley and Atkinson, 2007). Ethnography is therefore associated with the enterprise of giving 'voice' or revealing hitherto hidden aspects of the culture of a group, and is a particularly appropriate approach for understanding children's cultures and social networks (Jenks, 2000).

The first phase of the research, when the children were aged between three/four years old and six/seven years old, included observational study in the pre-school and school settings as well as interviews with teachers and carers and with parents in the child's home. With its large component of observational work, this phase was rather more traditionally ethnographic than the later secondary school phase. During the latter phase the main method was the semi-structured interview, used intermittently from ages twelve/thirteen through to age seventeen. Although, as I will be explaining, the term 'interview' does not quite do justice to the variety of activities and strategies that were included, and it is a rather formal term for what began to feel more like two-sided conversations, as the relationship and rapport developed between myself and the young people.

Selecting the children and getting to know them

At the beginning, I was interested in exploring how early social experiences prior to compulsory schooling might influence the child's socialisation into the environment of formal school and their emerging sense of self. So I arranged to visit a range of types of pre-school setting: one private nursery, one social services nursery, one pre-school centre attached to a primary school, a parent/toddler group, and the home of a non-nursery attendee (contacted through the waiting list of one of the primary schools). Through a combination of observations and informal chats with children, staff and parents in these settings, I arrived at a group of ten children: Anna, David, Ghita, Jayne, Kelley, Liam, Martin, Shelley, Simon, and Umar (the fictional names I gave them to protect confidentiality). The ten were selected partly because they were already committed to attend one of three local primary schools that had consented to participate in the study. This logistical consideration dominated the selection rather more than balancing socio-economic factors. One of the children was Asian-Indian, the others were white. In three cases the parents were both unemployed, in two cases one or both parents were within a middle class professional/managerial group, whilst in the remaining five cases one or both parents had traditional working class forms of employment. The ten presented an equal mix of boys and girls. A further narrowing down process was required for writing this book. The five children whose stories I present here, Martin, Shelley, Simon, Jayne and Liam, were chosen because they are the ones with whom I have collected the most data, over the longest time.

Gaining and maintaining consent

Ethical aspects of the research relationship needed some careful thought when I began and continued to be an issue throughout. Wolcott (1999) provides a down-to-earth view of ethical issues in ethnography which matches my experience:

> I do not present or defend ethnography as an ethical pursuit. It is, after all, the business of inquiring into other people's business. You can try to be ethical in how you go about doing that, but a basic question remains: Is it ever ethical to probe into other people's lives? I regard the underlying issue as one of balancing risks and benefits. My initial premise is that the individual with the most to benefit is always the ethnographer, and the individuals with the most to risk are *always* those among whom the ethnographer studies.

> The risks can be minimised, the benefits or potential benefits maximised, guided by practices of openness and disclosure. (Wolcott, 1999:284)

I was particularly concerned about the children's own choices about being involved. Issues about consent to participation in research are far from straightforward when working with young children and they are also particularly complex when working with participants over a long time. Most codes of research ethics emphasise the need for a participant to provide 'informed consent' (for example British Educational Research Association, BERA, 2004, and British Psychological Society, BPS, 2009). Even when working with adults this is a much more complex business than it at first appears, since researchers have to make difficult decisions about how much information to provide, knowing that the research brief frames all aspects of communication and behaviour.

When working with children, especially very young children, these difficulties are compounded. They are complicated with regard to children's capacity to be informed, that is to understand the demands of the research, and to give consent, that is to enter into verbal negotiation about participation. Consequently, ethics codes identify parents and teachers as the gatekeepers of consent for research with young children. I recognised that it was important to gain consent from all the parents of the participating children but I also felt that it was important to try to give some control to the children themselves by explaining my presence in their lives in a way they could understand. I also knew I would be able to explain the aims of the study more clearly as they grew older, with a thorough de-briefing session at the end. In actuality my briefings and debriefings became a continuing process during the course of the study.

In recent times a considerable body of literature on research with young children has challenged the idea that consent is a verbal agreement and has shown that a shy or anxious child, for example, might be withholding consent through clear non-verbal signals. The maintenance of consent is a further problem. If a young child begins an interview happily enough but then appears to become bored, tired or uncomfortable, the researcher needs to recognise signals that might indicate that the child is reluctant to continue. Lindsay (2000) discusses research ethics codes with regard to children and cites the CPA (1992) recommendation to be responsive to such behaviour. The concept of 'continuing consent' put forward by Lindsay is a more appropriate term to describe the ethical aspects of the research relationships in this study.

The longitudinal nature of this study raises ethical issues of its own. In their discussion of the ethics implicated in qualitative longitudinal research, Holland *et al* (2006) say it is important that 'the research relationship is not and does not become exploitative with the passage of time and the growth of familiarity and trust' (p28). Longitudinal studies, they say, expose the extent to which consent is a process rather than a single act and they caution that participants may feel coerced into continuation. So within ongoing longitudinal research continuing consent must be matched by a corresponding process of continuing information from the researcher as the children become more able to understand the aims of the study.

These consent issues are well illustrated by the story of my contact with Umar and his withdrawal at the age of thirteen. Umar's inclusion in the study was significant as he was the only ethnic minority participant, and also the only child who had not attended nursery pre-school provision, a significant factor during the first phase. My initial contact with Umar and his family was made through a home visit after the school had released the details of some of the children who were on their waiting list. I explained that the aim of my study was to explore how children settled into school, with particular emphasis on the social aspects of that experience. Umar's mother Zubeda appeared happy to help, and gave her consent for me to come into their home, observe Umar, and talk with him and herself. I had previously lived in their neighbourhood and had also undertaken some voluntary ESOL work with an acquaintance of hers, factors that may have contributed to the establishment of trust by the family. I only met Umar's father on one occasion, an event which seemed important as a further milestone along the journey of mutual trust.

When I resumed contact after the seven year break, Zubeda appeared perfectly willing to re-engage in the study. Umar too seemed happy and co-operative during the first interview at this stage. But when it came to arranging the second interview Zubeda informed me that he was reluctant to continue. She explained that Umar thought the study was too 'babyish'. This was a rather unclear explanation but it did seem consistent with the data I had recently collected with Umar, in which he expressed a strong wish to present himself as mature. I wondered if he felt that my involvement in his early childhood somehow cramped his style as a developing teenager. This was a particular loss to the study as I had hoped to explore his awareness of his ethnicity as an aspect of his identity, especially given his ethnic minority status within both his primary and secondary school. Although this was a blow there was nothing I could do about it. I had to respect his wish.

A triangular relationship

Of course it was not only the young people that I formed a relationship with during the period of the study. I also got to know parents, mainly mothers, who to a certain degree acted as gatekeepers to their children's participation. I interviewed the parents on several occasions during the early phase of the study, because I wanted to set their perceptions of their children against the information I was gaining from the children themselves and from pre-school and school staff, as a form of research triangulation. Parents were still the gatekeepers of children's participation when I re-established contact after seven years. Again, it was important to feel that I had both the consent of the children and the support of their parents. During the first interview that followed the seven year gap, I commenced with a co-constructed drawing of a time-line of the significant events that had taken place since my last visit. This was done in the presence of a parent, as part of the intention behind this activity was to provide an emotional safety net in the case of disclosure of any upsetting incidents or changes. In some cases, though, the parent dominated the activity and rather swamped the young person's own account of events.

In one or two cases the parents' own reasons and agendas for their children's participation became apparent. David's mother, for instance, told me that she hoped David might 'open up' about the grief he felt on losing his grandfather by talking to me. I had to explain that I was not a counsellor and recommend appropriate professional help. I had to be attentive to the dangers of coercion, especially in the light of the longitudinal nature of the study, but I was also aware that coercion could sometimes come from the parents. In contrast to Umar's mother, who acted as an advocate for her son in presenting his wish not to continue, I sometimes felt that parents' generosity in helping me with my research might have dominated their children's feelings about continuing. For example, Simon's mother Kath was enthusiastic about the family's involvement in the study but I wasn't so sure about Simon himself. It was a relief when Simon appeared very willing to talk further with me at age seventeen, and was very forthcoming in our conversations, as by this time I had ceased to use parents as gatekeepers for continuing consent.

Participant involvement: incentives and understandings

Perhaps rather than attempting to understand why Umar wished to discontinue the study, a better question is why any of the children wished to continue. What did they get out of their involvement? This was an important ethical question to keep asking, a strategy for avoiding an exploitative relationship, in line with Wolcott's advice (1994). There are many answers. They vary from individual to individual and from time-phase to time-phase, and reveal the children's various understandings of who I was and what I was doing in their lives. After the sequence of interviews that took place at ages twelve to thirteen, I gave a reward in the form of vouchers for music and books. At other times the rewards were much less tangible, and I can only speculate about what they might have been.

In the early part of the study the children might have benefitted in two ways. They probably gained from the positive one-to-one attention, and secondly, this often took the form of play and fun. Though my role as participant observer varied considerably according to the time point of the study, the nature of the educational setting and the sociability of the child concerned, I certainly spent time engaging in activities alongside the children and playing with them. Any ethnographer of early years' educational settings has to make decisions about their level of engagement within the children's own worlds and it was sometimes difficult to decide whether to play with the children or to stand back and make field notes or video recordings – a dilemma recognised in discussion of ethnography by Emerson *et al* (1995). The term 'participant observer' so frequently used in the research methodology literature does not really capture the complexity of ongoing decisions about how far to engage and how far to observe at any particular moment during the course of the study. The participant observer role can be conceptualised as a continuum, with a high level of engagement at one pole and a 'fly on the wall' observer stance at the other. My understanding of this continuum, and the various decisions that might be made along it, were informed by accounts of childhood ethnographies such as those by Corsaro (2000), Sluckin (1981), Davies (1989), Paley Gussin (1984) and King (1984). I positioned myself at various points on different occasions to suit various purposes. For example I made the following note after a morning of observation in Simon's pre-school:

> Simon is engaged in solitary play, driving one of the playground cars. I start a conversation about his car (I've hardly spoken to him yet). I ask him if he needs any petrol and we get into a pretend game of re-fuelling the car. He seems to enjoy this and wants to repeat it several times over. He seems happy to interact with me in this way and has perhaps become used to my presence in the nursery over the course of several visits.

My intention on this occasion was to develop a role with Simon in which I would become a familiar presence in the nursery: an 'atypical, less powerful adult' (Corsaro and Molinari, 2000:180) or 'least adult role' (Mandell and Thorne, cited in Mayall, 2000:121). Simon seemed a shy child and I had not felt it appropriate to initiate a conversation with him up until this point. However, I was mindful of my plans to hold a series of more formal conversations with him so I needed to begin to develop rapport. In contrast, and at the least participative end of the continuum, I took up a passive stance as I observed David in the playground playing a dare-devil game with his mates in which the object seemed to be to run up the brick walls of the playground. This took place in a far flung corner of the playground, well away from the eyes of staff. I needed to keep a low profile at this point as David and his mates were probably well aware of the illicit nature of this activity.

Research with young children is more ethical if there is something in it for the children – if methods can be devised that will be experienced as enjoyable (O'Kane, 2000), and that minimise pressure and difficulty, for example high literacy demands (Christensen and James, 2000). Working with children requires a high level of creativity in devising research methods that can both access the data needed to fulfil the purposes of the study and also take these ethical demands into account. It is often those who work with children who pioneer innovative methods for use with older populations, enhancing the range of qualitative research techniques within the social sciences. Woodhead and Faulkner (2000: 30), for example, speak of a 'broadening' of psychologists' methods with children. Recent collections on research methods with children provide ample evidence of this (Alderson, 1995; Lewis and Lindsay, 1999; Christensen and James, 2000; Nutbrown, 2002; Lewis *et al*, 2004; Greene and Hogan, 2005). I devised a mix of various data collection strategies throughout the study, in an effort to balance this mix of aims by coming up with methods that would prompt self belief statements and statements about change and about changes in identity, but also ensure that these would be experienced as positive.

During the pre-school phase of the study I took a range of dressing up clothes for the children to select from. I believed this activity might prompt comments on matters relating to self, appearance and gender, and might also be enjoyed. Another strategy was to show the children, at age twelve/thirteen, the video recordings I had made during the early phase of the study when they entered the first year (Reception class) of school. The intention was to activate self reflection, initially by playing selected recordings without making remarks and then, if the child offered little comment, to follow this up with questions designed to prompt comparisons between 'then' and 'now', with a view to ascertaining which self beliefs had changed and which had remained consistent. Several of the children described this experience positively ('nice', 'good') when asked to reflect on it, though Jayne described a mixed bag of feelings: 'Quite nice. Embarrassing though'.

It was also important to create some variety of activity and not to present a barrage of verbal questions. Another visual stimulus was a pictorial representation of 'tree figures' used for purposes of projective identification (see Appendix 2). I was given this in a workshop during the late 1980s and have never been able to trace its source.

It is difficult to imagine what the children made of the study. Snippets of evidence give me some clues. During the pre-school and Reception class phase I overheard one child refer to me as 'the camera lady', as I was often to be seen with my video camera. Others were interested in the notes I was writing, recognising I was writing about them, and sometimes they wanted to add their own marks in my notebook, something that the teacher in me could not resist (see Corsaro and Molinari, 2000). During the adolescent phase of the study it was possible to glimpse the young people's understandings about it. An interesting insight into the way I was perceived by Martin, for example, came at the end of my final interview with him, at age seventeen. The ending of an interview, when the tape recorder has been turned off, offers opportunities for both participants to reflect on the interview experience. Martin made a brief but significant observation following the two dramatic revelations he had made on this occasion (see Chapter 6): 'You weren't expecting anything like that', he said. The comment suggested that he was aware of the unusual nature of his story, and that, perhaps he might have been aware of this as being rather a 'gift' for me.

A glimpse of participants' self awareness occurred when I contacted the seventeen year old Jayne a year after my previous conversation with her. I asked her: 'What's been happening since we spoke last year?' She replied 'Starting work. Nothing major'. Her rather surprising judgement about the relative insignificance of starting work possibly indicated she thought I might be after more 'major', perhaps more dramatic events. It may also have supported her negative perception of her job as unexciting. In a rather similar way, when I visited Shelley for the first time after the seven year break and constructed the time-line with her, Shelley's mother commented 'We're quite boring aren't we?' These brief observations indicate self awareness, an awareness of the impressions they were making on me.

Researcher reflexivity and emotional aspects of the research relationship

During the phase of data collection, within the ethnographic site, such as the pre-school classroom, or within the interview, the qualitative researcher must operate with self awareness, keeping an ear and eye out for recognising how each party is relating to and positioning the other, and she must continue to do this during analysis of data. As I read and analysed interview transcripts and field notes, or watched video footage from the early part of the study, I was conscious of the young people being aware of me being aware of them. It is through this research interaction, through this evidence of mutual self awareness, that we see the interdependence of the construction of self and others. Such glimpses show us the 'mirrored' self that Cooley spoke of, and the 'me' self that Mead writes about. We see that it is when we start to think about how we are reflected in the minds of others that we become aware of self, reflecting the deeply social nature of self. It is at such moments that the methodological process of this study echoes its theoretical enterprise.

The researcher needs to look at themselves within their own research processes, deliberately searching for indications of the management of impressions, expectations and mutual positioning (Warin *et al*, 2007). This kind of sensitivity is known as researcher reflexivity; it is a cornerstone of qualitative research. A number of qualitative researchers have argued for this value. For example Morgan (1981), Atkinson (1990), and Coffey (1999) claim that when the researcher writes their own self into their ethnography they bring much greater authenticity to it. This value is based on a strong tradition of feminist writers who have challenged traditional positivist research methodologies, arguing that what passes for objectivity in 'hygienic research' is inauthentic, a way of writing the personal and subjective out of the research process (Spender, 1981; Roberts, 1981; Stanley and Wise, 2002). Through this feminist critique of the illusion of objectivity, feminists have not only admitted and acknowledged that the researcher is emotionally and relationally involved and exerts an influence on the processes and outcomes of data collection, but also that they have moved one step further and positively encourage awareness of the researcher's subjective involvement. Harding, for example, advocates 'strong objectivity' (1993) in research, turning the traditional positivist value for objectivity on its head in order to emphasise the need for reflexivity. She recognises that, paradoxically, we gain more distance from the research process by exploring our own influences within it.

An important component of 'strong objectivity' or 'researcher reflexivity' is the recognition and disclosure of the emotional aspects of the research experience (Kleinman and Copp, 1993; Coffey, 1999; Lucey, 2001). In their discussion of the role of emotions in fieldwork Kleinman and Copp emphasise that when researchers lack awareness of their emotional responses they are likely to be more influenced by them. Several aspects of these children's lives, certain interests and preferences, reminded me of my own childhood. Some of the experiences I was privy to, and the things I witnessed in the growing up of these children, also reminded me of my own children, who are only a few years older. Hunt (1989:9) draws attention to the ways that 'unconscious processes structure relations between researcher, subject and the data gathered', whilst Raphael Reed (1996) reminds us that '... we bring with us to our enquiry a set of issues, ways of looking and stories of sense-making which are profoundly affected by 'knowledge' and significances we carry in our unconscious' (p9).

A strong emotional response I often experienced during the study and continue to experience as I reflect on these young people is of immense gratitude. As the children grew up and became more capable of making a choice to remain in the study or to withdraw, I felt increasingly grateful for their continuing consent and trust. Did I have favourites? Yes, and my preferences tended to relate to my observation above regarding gratitude. The children who seemed most prepared to co-operate and were most generous with their time and their trust were those I was inevitably most attached to.

Conclusion

We can see that self awareness becomes the researcher's best tool for collecting and analysing data in a rigorous manner within qualitative research. This core value within qualitative research methodology has informed the carrying out of this study, as far as possible. It is not always easy to live up to this intention and I have no doubt I have been subject to many blind spots. But it is certainly an approach that is consistent with the focus of this study on self awareness as an educational goal.

Summary of Section 1

This section ends with a distillation of the key theoretical points and values set out in the preceding Chapters, ideas that re-appear within the following five stories as they unfold:

- The self is social. The capacity to tell a story of self is both derived from social relationships and facilitates their formation and progression. This suggests that relational rather than individual awareness has value as an educational goal

- The self is changeable. The capacity for telling a story of self will benefit people more than the creation of a strong sense of self. This is a subtle but important difference. Emphasising the capacity for self narration is a way of synthesising the chameleon and the snail models of identity presented earlier. It suggests the need for adaptability of the self as it changes according to the social context. However it also suggests a value for the ability to integrate different selves into a coherent and continuing narrative

- Identity formation and group formation occur interdependently as groups are created on the basis of beliefs about peers who are 'like me' and peers who are 'unlike me'. The formal and informal groups of the school system intensify these processes

- The need or desire to narrate self can be activated in a number of ways. The experience of dissonant identities can prompt the creation of an expanded story of self that can accommodate competing selves. This is believed to be a particular feature of adolescence, when there is recognition of different selves in different contexts. Fateful moments such as school transitions create both the need and the opportunity for identity narratives and operate as catalysts to activate the ongoing story of self

- Theorising the self as a capacity for making and remaking stories offers a critique of fixed or entity ideas about the nature of identity. Stressing a person's capacity to remake stories of self is linked to the developing theoretical critique of infant determinism. Qualitative longitudinal research can remind us to be wary of simplistic causal links between childhood and adulthood experiences. This critique of psychological determinist approaches to the lifespan is related to a value that arises out of the discussion of the childhood revolution; namely the importance of acknowledging and appreciating children as the people they are in the present moment rather than the people they are to become

- The capacity to create an identity, described here as the capacity to tell a story of self, and closely related to current ideas about the value of emotional literacy, provides a form of social advantage or identity capital. This means it should be equally available for all children.

Section 2
Matching theory with real lives: five stories of self

Setting the scene for the stories of Martin, Shelley, Simon, Jayne and Liam

I have used my interactions with the children in this study to cast light on theories about the construction of identity. At the same time, I harnessed theories of identity to help me understand the children. So the five stories that follow have been written with this interdependent duo of intentions. I wanted to gain a greater depth of understanding about the nature of personal identity and its development by exploring it in detail, with each individual, over a period of many years. I also wanted to portray a detailed picture of the interpersonal and intrapersonal lives of each of five children through their childhood and adolescence. The outcome of this latter intention is a set of entirely separate stories of self. Each shows how the young person has developed the capacity for self awareness, as they reveal the ways they are telling stories of self, and the different kinds of stories they are telling.

An overview of key background information about each of the children can be found in Appendix 1. It includes such details as the type of housing each lives in, parental employment and family composition.

6

Martin's story: a value for authenticity in telling a story of self

Introduction

According to most measurable indicators of social advantage such as material wealth and parental attention, Martin had a privileged childhood. In my exploration of how Martin constructed his story of self I was particularly interested to see how these aspects of his life were interwoven with a prominent feature of our conversations: his strong value for an authentic, 'true' self and his assertion that he consistently remained the 'same person' throughout the course of the study. This repeated emphasis was much more strongly expressed by Martin than by the others. It seemed to be rooted in a noticeable self consciousness that was apparent during his early years. In early adolescence he was sensitive to the idea that others perceived him in a way that jarred with his own sense of self. This misperception by others, as he saw it, confirmed his wish to be 'true' to himself.

I was not sure why this idea was so much stronger for Martin than for the other children. I followed the lead of theorists who have speculated about the relationship between social class and the development of a strong identity. Their arguments emphasise children's access to certain types of language, especially emotional vocabulary – ideas that are associated with the development of emotional literacy (Weare, 2004). Martin's emotional literacy was clearly on display in our conversations, especially as he grew older. In particular he communicated emotional courage about being himself despite possible bullying or rejection. His story contains features that are of considerable interest in themselves, such as his tale of the discovery of his real Dad, and his account of coming out. Interesting as these accounts are in their own right, I have also explored his narratives of these episodes to see how they answer my overall questions about the purposes and processes of identity construction.

I begin by presenting the young Martin as I got to know him during his pre-school year, aged four, and then during his first two years of formal schooling. I focus particularly on the observations about him that relate to his self consciousness during this time, a concept that is clearly implicated in the development of identity. Our first meetings took place at the private nursery he attended, Hazel Grove. It was situated in a pleasantly leafy location on the edge of town, with a spacious garden of mature trees and lovely views of the neighbouring countryside. It was conveniently close to Martin's home in a newly built executive housing estate. When we first met he was attending the nursery five mornings a week and was looked after by a child minder for the afternoon whilst his parents were at work. His mother Karen worked as a lending officer in a nearby bank and his father Andrew as a bank manger in a neighbouring town. At this stage of the study Martin experienced the life of an only child for much of the time, as his younger sister Rachel was only born when he was five. However, he was also positioned as the youngest of three, when his older half-brother and half-sister were around (see Appendix 1).

'He likes being centre-stage': Martin's self consciousnesses and self confidence as a young child

It was Martin who described me as 'the camera lady'. This observation is good place to start, as I believe that this awareness of me as an observer of him was strongly related to his emerging sense of self. The notes I made during my first series of observations of Martin in Hazel Grove show that he was very much aware of my presence in his world. When I look back at my video recordings of Hazel Grove and his first days at Bath Square primary school, I notice that he was often looking directly at the camera and seemed more aware of me than the other children were. I believe there were two reasons for this. Firstly, Martin was very interested in the camera I used. When I commenced the study I used an extremely large and conspicuous video camera borrowed from the university where I was based. Only later did I buy a less obtrusive one of my own. Martin wanted to look at the camera and understand how it worked.

> Martin gets absorbed in the water toys. Then he looks around himself at the others in the room. He notices me and his gaze stays on the camera. (Field notes, Hazel Grove nursery, March, Visit 1)

> Martin is sitting with the other children waiting for a drink. He is looking at me and at the camera, in which he seems very interested.

Later:

> He looks at the camera with total fascination. 'What's that?' he asks me pointing to the dangling lens cap. (Field notes, Hazel Grove nursery, March, Visit 2)

Martin, I soon found out, was very interested in computers and I linked his interest in the technicalities of my camera with his evident interest in computers, an aspect of his life that was supported by evidence from his Mum and the school staff. I noticed that one of the first objects he played with when he started in the Reception class of Bath Square primary school was an old camera, from which he became inseparable during his first day. In my field notes I commented: 'He relies heavily on the camera and the toy telephone. These things seem to give him security'. The camera became a rather useful socialising device for him, as he could pretend to photograph new classmates and thereby begin social interaction with them.

> Mrs Jones takes an old camera over to Ben, who is sitting with Martin in the home corner. The two boys have been playing with a telephone but Martin is now monopolising this and I imagine she brings the camera so Ben can have something of his own to play with. Martin is very interested in this. 'Oh – it does flash' he says. He persuades Ben to swap. He takes lots of pretend photos. Ben makes repeated attempts to get the camera back. Martin goes off on a wander round the classroom taking photos of most of the other children. (Notes from video recordings, Bath Square Primary School, September, Visit 1)

In my field notes later the same day, I wrote: 'He picks up the camera again and repeats his earlier activities including taking photos of me'. At home time: 'He takes the camera over to show his mother'.

The second reason for Martin's awareness of my presence in the classroom was more relational and linked to his sociability. It was when I came to analyse my video data, watching all the recordings I made of the children during pre-school and the first days of school, that I became aware of a particularly pro-social aspect of Martin's behaviour. His gaze was often directed outward to other children, watching them or engaging in play and talk with them. The video recordings show that some children were much more inclined to gaze downwards, absorbed in a toy or activity in their hands or close to them, whilst others were more likely to look around them, their gaze following the movements of their peers or in some cases the staff. Simon, for example (Chapter 7), was often absorbed in using construction bricks and piecing them together, perhaps playing alongside a peer but gazing down, engaged in his own activity. I return to this comparison of the children's gaze behaviour, and its significance regarding the beginnings of social understanding, when I discuss Shelley's first days of school in Chapter 6. Of the children who were more outward looking, some were more likely to be focused on other children and rather oblivious to adult staff and carers. Martin, however, seemed interested in the adults as well as the children and I noticed he appeared at ease communicating with staff as well as with his peers. His social curiosity and ease of communication also extended to me.

Children who are drawn to first observe and then interact with others have a head start in developing the mutually reinforcing concepts of self understanding and the understanding of others, that I call 'relational intelligence' and sometimes 'relational awareness' (see Chapter 3). I noted the pivotal change in the development of self that occurs when a person begins to form ideas about who they are, based on their understandings of the opinions that others hold about them (cf Cooley, 1902; Mead, 1934 and Harter, 1999). The beginning of this significant human understanding, this change in consciousness, starts with the recognition that one is observed by others.

I believed that Martin was aware of me watching him and his term 'the camera lady' may have signified this sense of being observed. A recognition that others see you, notice you and listen to you, is a necessary forerunner to the more developed understanding that others form impressions of you and make judgements about you. Martin, I felt, was quite often and rather more than some of the other children demonstrating his understanding that he was being observed. He was perhaps the most 'self conscious' of the children. He would quite often look at me before re-engaging in his activity, and this behaviour is captured in my video recordings.

During my pre-school visits I noticed Martin's capacity for making others laugh and his clear enjoyment of this effect. I felt it was further evidence of his developing social awareness. Judy Dunn's classic study (1988) shows that children's humour can provide evidence of the development of social understanding, as they are demonstrating an understanding of what will make others laugh. The following two extracts from my field notes of visits to Hazel Grove nursery show this:

> A group of children are seated on the carpet looking at books and waiting for a story. Harry, sitting directly behind Martin, takes Martin's head between his hands, opens his own mouth very wide and pretends to eat Martin's head. Martin looks at him and then ignores him. Then Harry pats Martin's head. Martin continues to ignore him and carries on 'reading' his book. After reading, aloud, for a little bit longer Martin puts his hands to the back of his head, turns around and again looks at Harry as if this has been a delayed reaction. Then he touches Harry quite roughly under his eye, pinching his cheek. Harry looks upset then repeats the same gesture on Martin's face. Ralph, sitting close to them, is now interested and the three engage in some rather deliberate poking and pinching of each other in a very slow and experimental manner. Then Martin pulls his eyes down with his fingers and makes a comical expression with his mouth, creating a 'funny face'. The other boys copy, and the three start laughing. (Notes from video recording, Hazel Grove nursery, May, Visit 6)

> Martin is sitting on the carpet between Anna and Vicky. Martin yawns. Then he says something in a funny, cartoon style voice. I don't quite catch the words – just the deliberately comic accent. Anna and Vicky laugh very loudly. (Notes from video recording, Hazel Grove nursery, June, Visit 8)

There was also evidence from Martin's mother Karen of his enjoyment of performing in public. Karen made several notes in the notebook I had provided for parents to record the day-to-day accounts of their child's new school experience, including a report of his delight at playing musical instruments on the stage in the school hall during a school assembly. In my interview with her at the end of his first year at his school, Karen told me 'He loves performing songs and impressions'. She mentioned this attribute again when I talked with her at the end of his second year of school:

> He is very confident. In fact he can be over confident sometimes. He was in assembly the other week reading out numbers and proud as punch. He likes being centre-stage. The Deputy Head asked him to do a solo in front of the whole school because he had heard him singing. He likes to perform the Spice Girls song to people.

This last extract presents the two sides of the 'self consciousness' coin. Most parents, like Karen, would surely feel some pleasure in being able to identify their child as 'confident'. Within Western conceptions of healthy child development, we tend to rate self confidence. Indeed I noted in Chapter 3 that the closely related term 'self esteem' is seen by many educators and psychologists as a panacea for all society's ills. So Martin's developing self confidence combined with his strong interest in others is surely a very good sign of the emergence of a 'strong sense of self', a quality that is increasingly prescribed as a goal of early years education (for example in the *Birth to Three Matters Framework*, Sure Start, 2005). However, Martin's mother suggests there is a rather fine balance between his confidence and what she terms his 'over-confidence'. Whilst she seems to be proud of his singing, an ability Martin developed later in his middle childhood when he sang in the church choir and became Head Choir Boy, her comment on the 'centre-stage' characteristic may have an element of disapproval. Karen's ambivalence brings to mind Emler's critique of self esteem and his suggestion that over inflated self esteem may be as much a problem as low self esteem.

Karen was not the only one to comment on Martin's enjoyment of being in the public gaze. A recurrent theme of my interviews with staff at Bath Square primary during his first two years was what they described as Martin's 'attention seeking' behaviour. For example, his first year teacher Mrs Jones gave me her interpretation of a singular aspect of Martin's behaviour, something I had observed several times myself, namely his tendency to lie down and sleep:

> One of the things he does, you've seen him, he sleeps here, or not sleeps. I don't know. Sometimes he's fast asleep. Sometimes he just needs that – close-down – or he's doing it so somebody will come over and be quite loving to him and say 'Oh, are you alright Martin?' Because when he first started doing it, the others were so nice with him and 'aah!' and put soft toys around him or went over and stroked him. So it could be he's doing it for a nice re-ward [laughs]. I asked the nursery people [staff at Hazel Grove] and they said he used to lie down at nursery a lot... But they said he used to watch to see if somebody was coming over to him. So they thought he might be doing it to get some attention.

At the end of his second year his class teacher Mr Hardcastle also mentioned his attention-seeking:

> He's always got to be telling me something and he's always got to put himself 'me first'. 'It's me'. I want to tell you first and I want to have your attention straight away for ten minutes when I arrive in school.

Martin's enjoyment of public performance seemed to come from a wish to make others laugh, as well as a love of singing and music. However it was also perceived by adults in his world as an attribute that was mixed with his need for attention. Attention seeking is disapproved of by early years' school staff, especially during the Reception class year when an implicit moral goal of schooling is to adapt to being part of a larger group of peers and to share resources, especially teacher attention (Maclure and Jones, 2009; Brooker, 2002; Fabian, 2002). This study includes other examples of strong teacher disapproval for children who find this difficult, for example in Shelley's story and Liam's (Chapters 7 and 10). For a child like Martin who had been 'top dog' in the nursery – the term used by his nursery staff to describe him – the adaptation to the larger group of children, and less frequent attention from teachers, was difficult, and staff were not very sympathetic. This so called 'attention seeking', whilst it might be disapproved of by early years' staff, shows Martin to be sufficiently socially skilled to understand how some of his actions were going to be responded to.

'I'm just the same person': Martin's value for the authentic self

Martin's self consciousness as a pre-schooler and young school pupil seemed to be linked to the phenomenon I found so interesting in the twelve year old Martin, when I met him again after the seven year gap in our acquaintance. This was his value for self consistency, for being authentic and 'true' to himself. This emerged in several forms during the sequence of conversations that took place in year 8, his second year at St. Stephen's secondary school. For example when I first met up with him after the seven year gap and we viewed the video extracts of his first days at school:

> JW: Do you sort of recognise yourself in that?
>
> M: I, sort of, but I know I looked like that but not now like when I'm getting older, I just don't see myself to be that young, it's just really strange.
>
> JW: Do you think you're sort of the same person or?
>
> M: Definitely, yes.

Then at a later point in the interview:

> JW: Are there some things that are different about you or some things that have stayed the same?
>
> M: Not really no, I don't really know but I know that I haven't changed, I definitely haven't changed at all, I'm just the same person

Martin's attitude to these questions was in marked contrast to others who were anxious to emphasise that they *had* changed, perhaps because they wanted to present themselves as more grown up. For example David and Umar, whose stories are not told in this book, drew attention to changes in the ways they dressed, their musical tastes ('writing raps'), attitudes to school ('not so into my work now') and increase in number of friends ('hanging around with my mates'). They wanted to present themselves firmly as teenagers and as fully aware of prevalent social scripts, subscribing to the culture of young males. Martin's agenda was altogether different. His assertion that he was unchanged also came from a desire to present himself well but in this case his ideal self seemed to incorporate self consistency as a strong feature.

As a believer in his unchanging nature, it was particularly interesting to find that he was also disturbed when he encountered a view of himself in the observation of others which appeared inconsistent with his own sense of his identity:

> Everyone knows me now [in High school] and everyone calls me Harry Potter and it drives me up the wall. I don't even look like him and even my friends think I look like him. It's really weird how people assume things that aren't true. (Interview 1, year 8, St Stephen's secondary school)

In Chapter 3 I referred to the difference between the 'I' self (the primitive self as 'knower') and the 'me' self (the more advanced self, as known and objectified). The various questions and strategies I devised for my interviews with the children when they were in year 8 were aimed to prompt self reflection, to construct the 'me 'self. For example, when I asked the children to imagine how they would come across to others and specifically imagine the perspectives of three key people in their lives, some children found this challenging (see Liam's story, Chapter 9). Martin's comment quoted above, is a nice example of an *unprompted* demonstration that he was constructing a 'me' self. He was clearly aware of the views others held about him. However, in this case there was a jarring or dissonance between his own ideas about himself and the perceptions of others. Elsewhere I have used the term 'identity dissonance' to describe this kind of jarring (Warin *et al*, 2006; Warin and Dempster, 2007). Identity dissonance can create an important turning point within a process of self construction because it has the effect of revealing particular valued perceptions about self. Martin believed that this perception differed from an underlying truth about him, providing evidence of his faith in an authenticity of self.

Although Martin gives us a sense of how he *doesn't* want to be portrayed, we do not see quite how he *does* want to be portrayed. After all, some people might be pleased by the Harry Potter comparison. Later in his interview, however, he cast some light on the Harry Potter problem:

> There's quite a lot of people in our school and they're not very, I can't say the word actually, it's like they're quite clever and everything and they know what to do and everything but they don't have as many friends and I think that's wrong. It's like I always go up to them and say 'oh hi how are you' and everything but I normally hang out with my best friends.

Martin can be seen here positioning himself within the still comparatively new school, comparing himself with others, particularly in terms

73

of key categories of cleverness and popularity. The speech is a nice illustration of Pollard's observation of children's coping strategies as they try to achieve an appropriate balance between maintaining their peer group status and satisfying school goals (Pollard, 1987). Pollard's study of 'Goodies , Jokers and Gangs' shows how important it is for children to identify themselves with others so they have a group identity that gives them a feeling of belonging. This implicates identifying their own group to explain what attributes are shared, and identifying the attributes of other groups to emphasise the differences between groups and consolidate group boundaries.

This process is well recognised by social psychologists such as Tajfel (Tajfel and Turner, 1979), who describes it as the formation of ingroups and outgroups. It is a crucial plank within processes of identity formation. Identification with a group implicates beliefs about self and about others in the group through social comparison. Sociologists are more likely to use the term 'othering' to describe the same process, for example Hey (1997), who applies it to the processes by which secondary school girls form groups and sub groups.

In the extract above, Martin is 'othering' the people who are 'quite clever'. He seems to have rather ambiguous feelings towards these people. It is interesting to speculate what word he is searching for and why he can't say it. Perhaps he is thinking of 'nerd', which is often used by his age group to characterise precisely the sort of people he seems to be describing, Harry Potter types perhaps. On the one hand he seems to want to dissociate himself from them, preferring the company of his own best friends who 'hang out' together. Yet he also feels drawn towards such people because he seems to feel sorry for them and also to experience some moral indignation on their behalf, as he suggests it is wrong that they don't have friends. He seems to be aware of the difficult balancing act between cleverness and popularity that means these 'quite clever' peers don't have as many friends as he does.

The need for friends and popularity emerges clearly as a strong value in this interesting extract. Martin says it is 'wrong' that the 'quite clever' people don't have friends. This moral indignation and the subsequent conscious kindness that he tells me about is a strong part of Martin's story of self that I say more about below. So in this careful self construction and self positioning around the concepts of Harry Potter, cleverness and popularity, we see Martin being clearly and explicitly reflective about who is he is, constructing his story of self.

Martin's statements about self nicely illustrate Harter's description of the development of self in middle adolescence (Harter, 1999). Her approach to identity formation is in line with Erikson's idea that the main goal of development in adolescence is to construct a coherent identity that integrates disparate selves (Erikson, 1980). Harter presents an illustrative monologue which portrays the anxieties of a girl consciously trying to reconcile the various facets of herself as she experiences them in different social contexts: with her close friends, with a larger group of friends, with her mother, with her father, with both parents together, and with potential boyfriends. The monologue ends: 'So I think a lot about who is the real me, and sometimes I try to figure it out when I write in my diary, but I can't resolve it. There are days when I wish I could just become immune to myself' (p68). Harter's example is consistent with my term 'identity dissonance', where the co-existence of different selves prompts an emotional need for finding the 'real me'. Of all the children in the study, it was really only Martin who seemed to typify this kind of explicit self reflection.

The data I collected with Martin allows me to explore the socio-emotional experiences that prompt a telling of self. We have seen that this can be through an experience of dissonance when different selves are experienced in different social contexts and there is a desire to synthesise them, or when there is a feeling of being misunderstood and misrecognised. A related prompt for the telling of a story of self arises when others describe you in insulting or bullying ways. Bullying, or the fear of bullying, can act as a strong prompt to defend the self. We see this kind of entrenchment in the following account from Martin, where he appears to feel the need to defend the quality of his supportiveness to his friends. He is perhaps worried about being seen as too much of a goody two shoes:

> I think I'm always like that, nothing changes with me, I'm always there for people and they're always there for me whenever, and they're just like, they're just like my friends and I'm supporting them in every way ... I don't care what other people think of me cause I'll always support people ... I don't really care if people call me names, I just ignore them. They don't do it often but say if

someone is crying and I help them, they're always like 'oh you're such a supportive' but I'd rather choose them than being like, stay brave and everything.
(Interview 1, year 8, St Stephen's secondary school)

In this extract, Martin adopts a strong moral stance. He presents the unchanging nature of his identity as a defence against name calling. He
portrays himself as the possessor of a strong, consistent and defended
sense of self. It is interesting to speculate about why he has a much
stronger and more explicitly articulated value for an authentic self than
the other children in the study, why he appears to engage in more
identity work. Given that his background is the most middle class of the
children in the study, it is worth considering how social class impacts on
this value. Comparing Martin with the other children in the study has
led me to question the extent to which an ability to tell a differentiated
story of self is connected to social class. Skeggs (2004) asks whether the
production of identity is the prerogative of those who are privileged to
have the time and space to engage with it. The activities implicated in
self reflection and self construction, she argues, pre-suppose access to
cultural resources, techniques and practices necessary for producing
and knowing a self, and these are not available for all. Coté (1996) also
acknowledges that a higher social class background provides advantages in constructing identity through access to greater opportunities
for reflecting on and communicating about self, defining such advantages as identity capital, the extent to which a person invests in who
they are. Children like Martin may have privileged access to particular
discourses and vocabularies that enable a richer and more elaborated
story of self.

Martin's emotional literacy

During the sequence of interviews that took place during year 8 there
was plenty of evidence of Martin using a rich emotional vocabulary. He
seemed to relish discussion of his relationships, especially his highly
valued relationship with his 'best friend', of whom he said 'we're always
there for each other'. He used emotional words such as 'sensitive' to describe himself on several occasions during these three interviews, for
example: 'I'm very sensitive about my friends and everything and my
family'. A question about the quality of the relationship with his Mum
compared with his Dad prompted a statement about his love for his
parents and his equal loyalty to both: 'nothing changes in how I love

them the most'. Love was a word he used readily, including portraying his relationships with teachers: 'I love the teachers. They're funny and stuff'.

Martin also showed emotional literacy in the fluency with which he described himself when I prompted him to 'bombard me with words that describe you', the research strategy described in Chapter 5. He quickly produced a list of personal attributes. These were extremely positive: 'Kind, sensitive, clever, sharing, happy.' What is more, he could elaborate on each attribute when asked to do so. He was also capable of switching perspectives and imagining how he came across to others. In all these ways, he displayed a high level of emotional literacy. Did he have this facility because he was more middle class? I believe he had developed a rich resource of emotional vocabulary through exposure to it within his family and his school. It might be significant that the explicit altruistic moral values present in the ethos of St Stephen's school, which selected children on the basis of their Christian religion, were consistent with the values of Martin's family.

More needs to be said about Martin's strong value for helping others, a theme that emerged during our talks. For example, when I asked Martin to identify himself with figures on the tree diagram that I used during the year 8 interviews (Appendix 2) he chose number 7 because 'I just like helping people'. He went into more detail in the follow-up interview: 'I know a lot of people and if they're discomforted or like really quite upset about something I always talk to them and everything'. As he explained in the extract quoted above, he was prepared to risk unpopularity with peers in order to defend and befriend an unpopular classmate. He had a strong identification with his family's values for 'helpfulness towards others' which was connected to their explicit Christianity. At the age of twelve, he was open about this aspect of his life when he rationalised his choice of secondary school on the basis of his religion. But at age seventeen he told me he had rejected his family's religious views. Martin's idea about the importance of an authentic self seems likely to be something he has absorbed as part of his family's values and within his school, which reinforced them.

Another important influence on Martin's display of emotional literacy concerns gender. An interesting dimension of the interviews conducted with Martin during his middle childhood concern his apparent gender flexibility and his awareness of gender issues, for example in his quite frequent use of the term 'sexist'. Several times during this sequence of interviews he told me he enjoyed good friendships with girls at school and preferred to participate in mixed gender peer groups rather than all male groups. He also told me how much he disliked the 'hard boys', and rugby. He was explicit about his enjoyment of watching romance films with his mother and recognised this as something that many boys would not want to do. He dissociated himself strongly from his father's love of football. He seemed to be willing to fly in the face of gender prescriptions for boys to be less 'emotional', and to be well aware of this agenda, combining this awareness with the moral courage to dare to be different. His openness to reflect on and communicate about his emotional life increased his emotional literacy. It also prepared the ground for his later choices about his sexuality.

Relational intelligence – Martin aged seventeen

Martin's emotional literacy, especially in the form of his vocabulary was even more evident when I interviewed him at the age of seventeen. The first topic of conversation between us concerned his decision to remain at St Stephen's for 6th form A-level study rather than move to a local college of further education, as many of his friends had done. He portrayed himself as a mature decision maker, balancing parental advice, teacher advice and the influence of his friends:

> After my GCSEs I was thinking a lot about it and at first I really didn't want to go into A-levels; I don't know, too much pressure and stuff. I preferred to go to college where all my friends went to, but I thought like, having a word with my parents and stuff, it was the best thing to do. I think that now it was the best decision to make... It is a difficult; it's like a transition period when you think you don't know what to do, because you haven't really got advice.

His concern about a lack of advice indicated that he recognised the independence of this decision process. His use of the phrase 'transition period' was particularly arresting, suggesting he was observing his own behaviour and had some awareness of it as a phase of life in common with others in late adolescence. It suggested a consciousness about his explicit narration of the story of his life to me as audience.

Martin approached this particular interview having clearly made a conscious decision to confide in me about two highly significant, emotionally charged developments in his life that had occurred since we last met. He was ready to plunge into an account of these early on in the interview:

> I've got two main events that come to mind, but one of them's quite confidential, but I'll tell you, that's absolutely fine... I found out that the man who I'm living with isn't actually my real father.

He proceeded to give me an account of the way that this emotional bombshell had been delivered to him by his dad Andrew or rather, by the man he had always believed to be his Dad. He states his emotional responses clearly:

> We [himself and Andrew] went on a bike ride to Moss Mere, and it was just me and him, and he just sat me down and told me. And I was so shocked, I just couldn't believe it.

Martin then related how he had followed up this news by investigating the family filing cabinet in the garage, discovering divorce documents, and tracking down his biological father, Terry. He then told me, in considerable detail, about the way he had contacted Terry. I give a brief overview of this episode and emphasise the aspects that specifically concern his construction of self, such as his portrayal of the emotional effort it involved: 'I was pushing myself just to try to find him'. The day came when Martin steeled himself to phone Terry:

> I directly rung his house one night. ... I picked up the phone. Just did it ... he answered the phone and I said 'Hi, it's Martin, I've finally got in contact with you'. And he started crying ...

Then Martin described the carefully planned meeting with Terry in the town centre, in which he was aided by his friend Aidan, who monitored the meeting from a distance until a secret thumbs up sign from Martin. These actions were undertaken without the knowledge of his parents, until finally Martin revealed to them he had met Terry and they agreed that he could maintain contact. He described the meeting with Terry's family, the grandparents he never knew he had, and his step siblings:

> Uncles, aunties, everything. Everyone was at the house; it was like a set up. It was horrible. I walked through the door and everyone was crying, cause it

must have been such an emotional time when they got divorced and that my mum got custody of me. So, everyone was just in my face and crying and hugging me, and I just didn't even know who these people were and they were just so shocked to see me, and that was really, really difficult to take.

Martin continued the account, with prompting, to explain that the subsequent relationship with Terry was very unsatisfactory. Martin felt increasingly sidelined by Terry until, a year and a half before our conversation...

I just thought, right, if he doesn't want to bother. Leave him to it...I think that chapter's been closed in my life. I don't think I'll ever get in contact again.

Several features of this account stand out because they illuminate Martin's understanding of self combined with his understanding of others, the twin phenomena I am conceptualising as relational awareness. The first concerns his relationship with his Dad, Andrew, and his discussion with me about which father he considered to be the 'real' one.

I still call him Dad to this day, because he is actually my dad, because he's looked after me ... My biological father, Terry, I never considered calling him Dad because he hasn't been there for me or anything like that, but yeah, that was a very emotional time ... I've realised who my real dad is now but I think once I've seen him, I know who he is, I know what he's like and I know his family and I think that that's closed.

The second interesting feature concerns his construction of his maturity and his belief that he has attained greater wisdom. In particular this concerns how he has learnt to recognise the consequences of his actions:

If I found out now that the same thing over again, I wouldn't do it. Until I'm older, no. I've recently thought about that and I just wouldn't do that... I had a lot of confidence and I just didn't care at the time, but now I know the consequences of what could have happened ... say if it went wrong or say it wasn't the guy who I thought it was, say he was a mad man or something like that. Cause I've grown up and I've realised situations like that and I've heard things on the news and I wouldn't have done it until I was older. Sometimes I can't believe I was so young doing it but ... I wanted, I wanted to just get out there and meet him, I didn't even think of the consequences, what would happen, or anything like that.

His story about his fathers emphasises relational intelligence in two ways: reflectiveness about, and re-appraisal of, his relationship with Andrew, and the construction of himself as older and wiser.

Having narrated the discovery about his fathers, Martin made his next revelation and told me the story of his coming out. In this account, too, I was aware of an emphasis on the emotional aspects of this change, further evidence of his emotional literacy and relational awareness. His coming out story was also particularly interesting in terms of Martin's earlier expressed value for an authentic self, for choosing to be who he really is.

> M: Erm, sexuality. Yeah, erm, I'm gay and that was a huge chapter in my life. That was a very, very emotional...With my parents; very, very, very hard, very hard.
>
> JW: Okay, so tell me, tell me about that, when did you know about that?
>
> M: I don't know when I knew, it was something that was I could probably say I was about fifteen – fourteen, fifteen – when I realised, and I told my close friends and erm, like Miles, he's gay now, so that's really strange for us, but you don't know why. Maybe it's like a friendship thing, cause we were so close and after I came out he came out to me, like about a year later. But we, we always knew each other were, sort of mentally, I don't know what it was but we always kind of thought...

Martin emphasised the considerable trauma of coming out to his parents and his subsequent relationship difficulties with them during a process of mutual adaptation to this significant change. He explained that he had planned to come out to his parents in his own time but that when they discovered he had been using a false alibi to cover his visit to a boyfriend, he felt obliged to break the news. His parents were 'disappointed'. His dad 'doesn't accept it whatsoever', whilst his Mum 'is warming to it'. Initially, a year prior to our conversation, there was a very difficult time when he left home for a while to live with the family of a friend whilst his parents got used to the idea.

Martin's account of discovering his sexuality emphasised self discovery rather than choice. For example he suggested that this was something he 'realised' and something he had 'always' known. He knew he was 'mentally' gay and that his friend Miles was too. This was put tentatively: 'we always kind of thought', suggesting that the construction of a gay identity was increasingly recognised over a long period of time. It was also referred to as a kind of mystery, 'strange for us, but you don't know why' as if there was no rational choice involved. The implication is that his discovered sexuality is his destiny. We see this implicit belief in many accounts of becoming gay (Sedgwick, 1990; Phelan, 1993). I realise as I read the extract above that I subscribed to this idea myself in the questions I ask Martin: 'when did you know about that?' and 'how did you first really know?' I do not ask 'when did you *decide*?' Our shared assumption is that this identity has been there all along, waiting to be discovered. This idea is consistent with Martin's belief in an authentic self, the realisation of 'the self that he truly is' (Rogers, 1961) rather than a deliberate choice. It suggests a form of identity essentialism.

His loyalty to his 'true' self, including his newly discovered sexuality, became an important principle within his social relationships. He told me how he valued the support of friends, all the more perhaps because his parents' support could not be relied on. Echoing the words of the twelve year old Martin, he claimed not to care about the opinions of others, although his vehemence suggests the opposite might be the case. In this extract he presents a strong form of emotional courage, a loyalty to being his own person, defended against abuse and potential abuse:

> M: Through high school, when I did come out I got a lot of abuse for it... And I, I didn't really care about it because I didn't care what anyone else thinks. I could not care less about people bullying me, I couldn't. But as soon as sixth form hit everything changed. Everyone always talks about it and we just we get on so well. In fact, all the people that used to bully me I'm actually quite good friends with now. We sometimes go out to the cinema and stuff.

> JW: So you did get a bit of bullying, then?

> M: Yeah, from that, yeah. But I've, yeah, I've got these three best friends and we do everything together, absolutely everything, and we just love each other so much. Like, without them, like yeah I don't know what I would do; really hard.

Interestingly Martin was also appreciative of the support he experienced from teachers at St Stephen's as well as from his friends. His account of this source of support includes open statements about how hard this episode of his life has been.

> All my teachers know. They, they're fine with it, they're absolutely fine... Like some of them wouldn't really talk about it, some would, you know, cuddle you if you were upset, hug you and stuff. Cause that's happened a few times when I've come to school so miserable cause of home, cause it's so hard. It was at GCSE stage and stuff as well, so it was hard doing my exams and stuff.

Martin's emotional literacy, his clearly articulated values for an authentic self, together with his statements about helping others, combine to form an emphasis in his story on the importance of social relationships, a relational form of intelligence. What is the connection, I wonder, between his relational intelligence and the 'discovery' he made about his sexuality? His understanding of self and others may have provided the courage he needed to make this choice and it surely provides the basis for managing his social relationships effectively so he has support systems to cushion it.

Conclusions

Martin had a value for an authentic self. This gave him a strong identity, one that could be defended from attack in the form of bullying or temporary rejection by his parents. He constructed himself as somebody who was prepared to stand up for his beliefs and who possessed the emotional courage to remain authentic, 'true to self', when his identity was under attack, for example from bullies or from rejecting parents. His sense of self enabled him to dare to be different, whether in taking risks over goody goody behaviour or, rather more significantly, making choices about his sexuality. It may also have enabled him to defy the social script for young boys to resist emotional communication. We saw that Martin developed a wide and sophisticated emotional vocabulary, evidence of a much stronger emotional literacy than the other children showed, and it does seem likely that access to this kind of talk might be related to the resources of his family background, especially given the mutually reinforcing ethic of care for others that was present in his family, church and school.

Martin's story does support the idea that identity capital is more available to some young people than others. His gender flexibility, shown during early adolescence, meant he was open to reflecting on, and talking about, emotional aspects of his social relationships. However, I also believe it was a quality that was particular to Martin. His interest in and ability to communicate about his social relationships is a cornerstone of relational intelligence, a concept that can be demonstrated through his story where we see his value for an authentic self being linked with an equally strong value for helping others.

From the early phase of the study, Martin's social understanding was apparent: a mutually reinforcing awareness of self and of others. I was struck by his emotional maturity during his adolescence in relation to the creation of self and also to his pronounced motivation to help others. Advances in one area support advances in the other. The two interdependent advances bring about relational intelligence.

7
Shelley's story: a shaky school entrance and an ambitious exit

Introduction

Shelley's first year at school was a difficult one. She did not settle well and appeared to be aggressive towards other children. Yet in the home context she was perceived as 'no trouble' and 'caring'. Her story raises important issues about inconsistencies in behaviour between the social worlds of home and school and what this disparity means for the construction of self. It also challenges assumptions embedded within developmental psychology about the influences of early childhood experiences on later outcomes. Shelley's difficult start at school, far from becoming entrenched and dominating her school career, had become entirely reversed by the time she was at secondary school. When I caught up with her at the age of twelve, she saw herself as happy in school and popular with peers. By seventeen she had moved into a college of further education and had strong aspirations to attend university to pursue her new found enthusiasm for a career in the theatre. She had become a person with a strong sense of her future.

Two different Shelleys: home – and school

I begin this account of Shelley with some words of disapproval from her Reception class teacher, Miss Powell, at the end of her first school term at Bridge View primary school:

> Her behaviour is consistently bad ... she's always nipping, biting. She's always doing something and it's as frequent as every ten minutes some days. She's hurting other children.

This comment came as a complete surprise to me as this kind of behaviour was not something I had noticed during my observations of Shelley as she settled into school, nor during my four observations at the church pre-school playgroup, St Oswald's, she attended in the five months before school. Neither did this account seem in any way consistent with the portrait of Shelley I had gained from my interview with Brian and Tess, Shelley's parents. I was puzzled.

When I heard the teacher's words I reviewed the various impressions of Shelley I had formed up to then. One of the voluntary helpers at St. Oswald's had told me she was 'very shy' and indeed I had found her to be cautious and unsmiling when I first tried to interact with her.

> I ask if I can sit next to her in a vacant chair. I tell her that her T shirt is lovely. She doesn't smile and makes an almost imperceptible nod then touches the heart picture on the front of the T shirt. She looks uncomfortable. The children are being called to line up. Shelley is looking with rapt attention at my video camera. I take this cue to show her the way the lens opens up. She looks away. (Field notes, St Oswald's pre-school, May visit 1)

At St. Oswald's, I approached Shelley slowly and gently, borrowing a strategy from young children's own play and unobtrusively 'playing alongside' her until she appeared to be a little more relaxed in my presence. By the time I conducted my first formal interview with her, asking her about preferred toys, activities and playmates, she was able to co-operate and seemed more at ease with me. I became interested in her lack of interaction with other children, though, noting 'I still haven't seen her speak to any of the other children'. I also observed how much she seemed to enjoy colouring with crayons, and the various gluing and sticking activities that were on offer, often looking most at ease during such activities.

After my interview with her Mum, Tess, in the summer before Shelley started Bridge View primary, I added some further impressions to my emerging picture of her. I was struck by Tess's concern about her lack of social contact with other children:

Well I'm quite looking forward to her going to school, more than not, just to get rid of her [laughs] but because she's not with other children a lot and that bothers me... [Later in the same interview] Apart from at my brother's house I can honestly say that she doesn't play with a lot of children, which is a shame really. (Interview with Tess, July)

Tess explained that there were several reasons for Shelley's lack of interaction with children of her own age. Firstly, Shelley was her second child after a ten year gap and most of her own friends had children who were contemporary with her ten year old son, Shelley's brother Patrick (see Appendix 1). Secondly, Tess and Brian were very concerned about the dangers of playing outside their own safe house and garden. A ready-made peer group of children awaited Shelley in the immediate neighbourhood but she was not permitted to join them. Tess and Brian were disparaging of other parents who allowed children as young as Shelley to play on the streets unsupervised:

Loads of them play out but to me, I don't know if three and four year olds shouldn't be on their own. Now that's only my opinion. They can do what they want with their own children but for me, if they aren't old enough to cross the road they aren't old enough to play on it, at least that's my view. ... but as I say there are a lot of children on the street, on go-carts and that. It's up to them. She's allowed at the side bit but she's not allowed in the front garden. (Interview with Tess, July)

Many parents are fearful of traffic and 'stranger danger' and a public media-led debate is raging about parental over-protectiveness regarding outdoor play (Gill, 2007; Guldberg, 2009; Layard and Dunn, 2009). This debate was just beginning to catch the public eye when Shelley was four years old. Her home was situated in a reasonably quiet residential area of council houses, though her street was used as a rat run to access the nearby main road and there seemed to be a lot of cars about. Tess's clear disapproval of the more permissive parents was perhaps related to a consciousness of social class, an 'othering' of the children who play on the streets and the parents who let them. Her comments emphasise the superior responsibility of her own family. The outcome of these parental views was that Shelley had little contact with other young children.

My conversation with Tess gave me insights into Shelley's daily life and her close companionship with her father and mother, both of whom were at home every day and available to her. Tess's work as a seamstress enabled her to be at home whilst Brian's work as a builder had ceased after a serious accident left him unemployed and in receipt of a disability allowance. Tess seemed pleased with the companionable relationship that existed between father and daughter, suggesting Shelley 'had it a little better than normal kids because he's got more time and more patience'. One of the activities Shelley and her Dad did together was to visit visit his father, her granddad, twice a week in an old people's home. Shelley displayed a caring attitude towards him. They also went for walks along the nearby beach, 'walking for miles along the sand'.

Shelley also spent time with her older brother, ten year old Patrick, playing Connect 4, marbles, computer games, and drawing with him. Sometimes she was looked after by her elderly next door neighbour Maura. I formed the impression that she spent a lot of time in the company of attentive adults rather than with children of her own age and I was sympathetic to Tess's hopes that Shelley would find friends and playmates of her own age once she started at Bridge View. Tess saw no reason to doubt that Shelley would settle in at school: 'I think she'll love it. I honestly believe she'll fit in quite well'.

However, my video recordings of Shelley's first days at school do not show a child who was loving school. There is certainly an element of enjoyment, especially on the very first day when she wandered from one area of the large open plan reception class to another, looking as if she was relishing the freedom to explore and enjoying the novelty of the toys and activities that had been set out. I saw her smiling and made a note: 'It's like Christmas for her'. We noted Martin's pro-social inclination to direct his gaze outwards, and watch other children, often as a prelude to engaging with them. I contrasted this with Simon's interest in the toys, games and equipment of the new classroom environment. Shelley's initial look of enthusiasm was motivated, I believed, like Simon's, by the enticing material aspects of the well supplied classroom, which contrasted with the resources of her home. Unlike Simon though, I didn't see her getting absorbed in any activities. On the contrary she seemed to hover about, sometimes with her arms held out behind her in a kind of flying gesture. She looked as if she was enjoying the freedom to move but, faced with so much choice, was unsure where to alight.

After the first day, she often looked rather lost and unsure what to do. I noted that she made several bids for attention from the adults in the room but did not manage to engage them. She didn't use verbal strategies but relied on touch and was quick to give up when ignored, an interesting contrast with the attention bidding strategies of the other children. Other researchers of children's transition into school, (Kamler, 1999; Fabian, 2002; Brooker, 2002; Maclure and Jones, 2009) have pointed out the successful adaptation of children who recognise that adult attention must be distributed across the entire class. Such children understand that '*Learning to live in a classroom involves learning to live in a crowd*' as the famous classroom ethnographer Phillip Jackson pointed out (1968, p10). Children who transgress this deeply implicit and highly important classroom rule attract negative judgments from teachers (Maclure and Jones, 2009). As I had observed at St. Oswald's pre-school, here too Shelley was rarely focused on the other children. Only on day four did I spot her playing *with* Adam and Sadie, piling up bricks in a corner of the play house, responding to Adam's 'we need more bricks' and his 'I'm having my dinner now'. I noted 'Shelley is definitely playing with Adam. This is the first co-operative activity I have seen'. But although Shelley was rather slow to orientate herself to her peers in the new school environment, there was nothing in her behaviour to presage the aggression Miss Powell described at the end of her first term.

Miss Powell herself presented her account of Shelley's aggressive behaviour as something of a mystery, describing it as a change in behaviour that had occurred sometime during the term:

> My first impressions were that she was a lovely little girl, very well behaved, and maybe for the first two months she was. Now, trying to think back I can't exactly pinpoint when all the naughty behaviour began... There was a certain time, and I can't really pinpoint when it was, that she began to change and what I initially thought of Shelley was that she was a really well behaved girl. Suddenly she changed and she was nipping and biting and scratching, wouldn't share. I remember this because I had to ask her father to come in at home time and explain the things she'd been doing during the day. I was really shocked to get him in and quite embarrassed ...Well she'll even bite and they [the other children] end up with big teeth marks, quite deep teeth marks on their arms and hands.

This comment and similar comments throughout this interview were further supported by the school's 'incident book' in which Shelley's misdemeanours were recorded. My field notes from this time say:

> Miss P showed me the log book of incidents concerning Shelley that she has kept for the last few weeks. These note: 'swearing, kicking, stamping on somebody's foot, smacking'. In several cases the words 'for no obvious reason' are included next to the offensive behaviour.

Miss Powell went on to suggest that the change might have started at the time that the whole class came together after the initial two months of gradual phasing in of small groups into the Reception class (a strategy practiced in all the primary schools in this study). She wondered whether Shelley had begun to be influenced by a group of 'naughty girls', identifying Francoise, in particular.

Not once did I myself observe any signs of aggressive behaviour although I continued to note that Shelley did not interact easily with other children. So the extreme change Miss Powell had witnessed in her behaviour was something of a mystery. I wondered what Brian and Tess made of Miss Powell's views of their daughter's progress at school. When I interviewed them at the end of Shelley's first year they were, unsurprisingly, bewildered by this turn of events and confused about how to account for Shelley's apparent misbehaviour, which they had now been invited to discuss with Miss Powell on several occasions. This theme dominated our conversation. Tess was understandably defensive and suggested that Miss Powell was perhaps exaggerating:

> Of course we need to know if she's behaving badly but it seems as if they're picking up on every little thing. I don't understand why they've started to write everything down.

Tess questioned the strict surveillance that Shelley had been receiving and also the accuracy of staff perceptions: 'How can the teachers tell what's going on in the playground?' Tess and Brian showed me Shelley's end of year report after her first year of school. It was positive about her art work but said she 'has difficulties with sharing' and 'has good friends but frequently hurts them'. This must have been a troubling report for the parents of a five year old.

In Shelley's second year of school her aggressive behaviour disappeared. At the end of the year Mrs Holden, the year 1 teacher, reported that she had 'settled down' and was progressing well, making improvements in her reading as well as her social skills. She believed this was the result of placing Shelley and Francoise in different classes. 'It's been a success separating her from Francoise. We couldn't understand why she had this nasty side to her'. Tess and Brian were also of the opinion that Francoise had been at the root of the problem. Tess described the beginnings of this relationship:

> T: We were pleased to begin with when Shelley had struck up this friendship with Francoise but Francoise is – well the two of them aren't good for each other. What it is is that Shelley tries to protect Francoise. She is unusually small for her age.
>
> JW: Has she visited Shelley here?
>
> T: No. [emphatically] Francoise is – well – I don't know if it's fair to say she's a bad influence because I don't really know her.

During these first two years of Shelley's time at primary school I became intrigued by the disparity of the school perspective and the parental perspectives of Shelley's behaviour. It was almost as if two entirely different people were being discussed. At times I felt I was witnessing a see-saw of blame, as parents blamed school and school blamed parents. Brian was particularly critical of Miss Powell. When I spoke to him at the end of Shelley's second year of school when she was in Mrs Holden's class, Brian told me: 'she's come on smashing' and said of Miss Powell: 'She wasn't really a Reception class teacher. She was better with the older ones ... We think Miss Powell expected too much of them'. For her part Miss Powell was disparaging of the parents' protectiveness that had deprived Shelley of social interaction with other children of her own age.

Whilst it was a relief to all concerned with Shelley, including myself, that the difficult beginning of school had given way to a smoother ride in her second year I remained intrigued by her offending behaviour. I wanted to understand it in light of my interest in Shelley herself, and also to understand how the interesting conflict between home and school perceptions might illuminate wider concerns about young children's readiness for the start of formal schooling.

First, the impact of Shelley's relative lack of interaction with other children prior to starting school invites scrutiny. Although she attended St

Oswald's pre-school in the five months just before starting at Bridge View primary school, it was only for two mornings a week, and she had not managed to interact with the other children there. It is possible that with the readily available responsiveness to her needs by the attentive adults in her life, she was unpractised in verbalising these needs. Her lack of practice may have led to inappropriate ways of engaging with peers and a lack of social understanding. Miss Powell supported this view.

> A lot of it [bad behaviour] seems to occur because somebody is standing in front of her peg. She wants to hang something on her peg so instead of asking them to move, she'll nip or she'll bite them. She doesn't say anything.

Many young children bite. Greenman (1995) claims that such behaviour is developmental in nature, something all infants and toddlers will pass through to a greater or lesser extent and that it is therefore not something that should be blamed on parents or on the children themselves. In toddlers and pre-schoolers biting is often perceived to be a form of primitive communication, a way of getting attention or expressing frustration in stressful situations (Oesterreich, 1995). Of particular relevance to Shelley's case, Claffey, et al (1994) suggest that biting in young children is linked to inadequate attention from adults, a lack that Shelley experienced in the new context of school in comparison with what she was used to at home.

Secondly, it is worth considering Shelley's age in relation to her classmates and Miss Powell's expectations. If Brian was correct that Miss Powell 'expected too much' of the children in her class then Shelley, a July born child who was young for her class, may have been at a particular disadvantage. Much has been written about the disadvantages summer born children face when they are taught alongside their slightly older peers at a stage in life where the age gap can make a big difference to a child's intellectual, social and emotional maturity (Bell and Daniels, 1990; Daniels et al, 2000; Oates, 2009). In the UK there has been a long standing debate about the early age of the start of formal schooling (Edwards and Knight, 1994; David, 2001). This has become heightened in the UK since the Cambridge Primary Review (Alexander, 2010) challenged the recommendations in the Rose report (2009) to maintain entrance to school at the age of four. (The Cambridge Primary Review gives a clear overview of this debate.)

So Miss Powell may have expected too much from the young Shelley, especially with regard to her level of social understanding. At one point in my first interview with Miss Powell she gave a specific account of Shelley's inability to empathise with other children. However, rather than recognising this as a normal lack of competence in a four year old (see Chapter 3) she seemed to see it as a deficiency:

> She doesn't seem to see that she's bitten somebody and it hurts them. She can reason it out after a great deal of discussion but there's no automatic feeling that I shouldn't do this – it'll hurt someone.

A third influence on Shelley's behaviour could have been the style of play she was used to with her much older brother. I reported the companionable activities that Shelley and Patrick engaged in, as described to me by Tess, but Shelley herself told me she enjoyed fighting with her brother. Perhaps the physical interactions that involved nipping, scratching and biting, occurred during her attempts to translate a form of play that was acceptable and safe in the context of home, with a bigger, stronger older brother, to the very different context of school.

Finally, given the considerable improvement in Shelley's behaviour once she was separated from Francoise, it looks as if that relationship had been influential in her aggression. Tess and Brian certainly thought so. Seven years later when the family looked back at my video recordings and identified Francoise, Brian commented: 'A little china doll she was – but what a bugger – but she comes from a very rough family, very rough'.

It seems likely that the four factors identified here will have interacted together to produce the behaviour that so incensed Miss Powell and that appeared to get Shelley off to a bad start at school with regard to staff approval. Another interpretation is possible, however. This is that Miss Powell developed a particularly unfavourable opinion of Shelley which then escalated and coloured her attitude, perhaps rather unjustly scapegoating her for the naughtiness of a particular group of girls. Shelley's second year teacher, Mrs Holden, implied some criticism of Miss Powell when she told me that Shelley had been placed on a 'Stage One'. This is the first stage of the register of special educational needs, implicating a degree of close supervision, and used by staff at Bridge View to indicate poor school behaviour. Mrs Holden clearly disagreed

with Miss Powell's judgment about the degree of Shelley's 'bad behaviour'. As she explained to me: 'Her behaviour was not bad enough to
be on a Stage One. I just felt personally that it was a bit drastic for somebody for Reception to start off with'.

The legacy of the home/school conflict

The clash between school and home accounts of Shelley dominated my
reflections about her development of a personal identity. It raises deeper
questions about the lasting impact of problems experienced in early
childhood and provokes reflection about how identity is experienced in
different socio-cultural contexts, such as home and school. Psychologists, sociologists and others who have portrayed holistic pictures of
children's sociocultural worlds have become interested in their experiences of switching between home and school. In their classic study
of young children's language development at home and at school, for
example, Tizard and Hughes (1984) noted consistencies and inconsistencies between these two contexts. They found that discontinuities in
language use and cultural values were especially pronounced for children from working class backgrounds. In the US, Brice-Heath (1983)
trained teachers to become more sensitive to disparities for children between the cultural contexts of home and school. Gregory (1996) claims
that when children move between home and school they inhabit 'several
different cultures at once' on a daily basis (cited in Osborn *et al*, 2006:
422).

An interesting question emerges from this body of research which is
directly related to the development of identity. If there are inconsistencies between the cultures, language practices, rules and expectations of different social contexts, does a developing child become confused by them? Or do they simply disregard this experience of multiple
selves? Do they find that there are rules and expectations in one context
that do not translate to a different context, leaving them unsure of how
to behave? In telling Martin's story of self, I noted that the values of his
family and his school were mutually reinforcing. This is not always the
case, as Pollard and Filer (2007) show in their discussion of continuities
and discontinuities across home/school peer cultural discourses,
which Power *et al* (2003) also reveal in their examination of the educational pathways of middle class pupils.

Shelley's story appears to offer an interesting case for exploring this idea further because of the major clash of views held about her at home and at school. Her case allows me to examine how far she was disturbed by this conflict of views and what impact, if any, this had on her developing sense of self. Did Shelley experience a kind of identity dissonance through this clash of views?

One of the procedures I used with the children during their first years of formal schooling was the Pictorial Scale of Perceived Competence and Social Acceptance (PSPCSA) devised by Harter and Pike (1983) (see Chapter 4). This has a teacher rating scale alongside the child's own rating scale. I used this scale with Shelley aged five, in the second year of school, when her class teacher was Mrs Holden. Shelley's self perceptions are shown in Table 1, alongside Mrs Holden's judgements about her. The table just shows the items that make up the 'social acceptance' strand of the scale. Rating is from 'not very true' =1, to 'really true' =4.

The results show that Shelley had a very different view to Mrs Holden's of her social acceptance of peers . Given the history of her first year and Miss Powell's low opinion of her sociability, we might expect that if Shelley had known about and absorbed this teacher view of her, she would show low scores for the 'social acceptance' items. This was not the case. These results suggest that she was probably unaware of the concerns of her teachers and her parents, their frequent meetings and

Table 1. PSPCSA Child ratings and teacher ratings for Social Acceptance

Social acceptance item	Shelley's perception	Mrs Holden's perception
Friends to play with	4	2
Others share	4	2
Friends to play games with	3	2
Has friends on playground	4	2
Gets asked to play by others	3	3
Others sit next to you/her	4	2

the difference of opinion that occurred between them. Perhaps her very lack of social understanding protected her a little from her teachers' critical views. It also seems likely that Tess and Brian would have been cautious about passing on teacher criticism with which they disagreed, another reason why Shelley did not internalise the negative views of her sociability. But I had some interesting conversations with Shelley herself that show that she was very much aware of the need to be 'good' and not to 'fight', suggesting that she had taken on board a strong desire to maintain the approval of the significant others in her life after her rather problematic start in school. The following exchange took place at the beginning of her second year in school when she was five, and in Mrs Holden's class. I asked the rather testing question that I tried out on all the children:

> JW: Are there some ways that you've become different than you used to be?
>
> S: Be good.
>
> JW: Are you gooder than you used to be?
>
> [Shelley nods]
>
> JW: What naughty things did you used to do that you don't do now?
>
> S: Fight. Play with Francoise.
>
> JW: Any other ways you've become gooder?
>
> S. I'm being good now and no fighting and no playing with Francoise. (From interview at beginning of 2nd year)

A year later her explanation of her choice of friends shows that she was still emphasising the wish to be good, and disassociating herself from those who were naughty and who fought:

> JW: Which are your friends at school?
>
> S: Lindsey, India and Sharon.
>
> JW: Why are those three girls your friends? Why do you like them?
>
> S: Because they're not naughty.
>
> JW: And you like to be friends with good children do you?
>
> [Shelley nods]
>
> Why are they your friends more than, say, Rory, or Adam? Why do you not have Rory for a friend?
>
> S: Because he fights. (from interview at end of 2nd year)

It is difficult to come to a clear conclusion about the legacy for Shelley herself of the home/school conflict. At most it might have evoked a stronger need to stay on the right side of teachers and stick with peers who would reinforce teacher approval, a desire that continued into secondary school. It is not the case that this conflict created identity dissonance of the kind discussed in relation to Martin's attempt in early adolescence to reconcile opposing views of himself. Identity dissonance is a relevant concept when considering how adolescents may be motivated to draw together competing experiences of self (as suggested by Harter, 1999; Erikson, 1980) but not when considering the identity construction of young children who lack the capacity for abstract thought. The difficult start to school had left a lasting legacy of bitterness for Tess and Brian, however, as was clear when I spoke with them seven years later.

It was straightforward tracking Shelley down seven years after my last talk with her in Bridge View primary, as she was still living in the house I had visited originally. At this stage a research assistant, Janine Muldoon, was involved in the study too (see Chapter 5). I was curious to see whether elements of the old conflict between home and school would get communicated to Janine as a new audience for the family. They did. Janine's impression on meeting Brian and Tess was that they were still distressed by the difficult start Shelley had experienced in the Reception class of Bridge View and that they appeared to feel lasting resentment of Miss Powell. Watching the video recordings of Shelley in the reception class provoked their feelings of anger:

> Brian: We were very disappointed about that [the Reception class].
>
> Tess: It's actually funny to see this [video] cause she's totally different to what she was at home ... For me she's crying for attention, she's wanting attention there, for somebody to talk to her... And this is why we went through quite a time when we didn't know how to cope with it, when she started school, because Miss Powell had you in nearly every day [this comment was directed to Brian]. 'Shelley is hitting other children, Shelley is pulling hair, Shelley is bored in class, in a science lesson'. Brian said 'What do you mean a science lesson' and she said 'well we have science, English, maths'. Brian said 'She's four years old' and she'd only just gone four, she was four in the July and she started school in the September and I said 'What do you mean you do lessons with them?' They had nine different subjects. Then she'd gone into

the next class, and we went to the parents' evening and they explained how well Shelley was doing then and how she'd changed and the teacher [Mrs Holden] said they didn't even know that Shelley had been put on a behaviour record or register or something. This teacher said 'We can't understand why she was put on one' so we were really really annoyed.

Tess's comments contain her retrospective understanding of the problems that Shelley experienced, a view which, over the elapsing years, has crystallised into a much stronger criticism of the school, particularly of Miss Powell. Her three major criticisms were: firstly, Shelley had not received the attention she was 'crying out for', a view that was strongly supported by my own observations. Secondly, when she did eventually provoke some attention from staff, they lacked understanding; and, thirdly, the curriculum was inappropriate.

Tess's criticisms of the early years of schooling generalise interestingly to the current national debate about the nature and purposes of schooling for young children and the early years' curriculum. Since the time of Shelley's early schooling there have been significant developments in the UK. Since 2002 we have the Foundation Stage, with its six areas of early learning. Whilst these are quite broad and incorporate personal, social, emotional, creative and physical development, besides the more traditional literacy and numeracy, there is still much criticism of the impingement of the standardised school testing that accompanies the national curriculum and forces early years' teachers to prepare pupils for what lies ahead (see David, 2001).

Tess and Brian have been left with a legacy of frustration through their contact with the school during the all important phase of transition into the school system. Tess sums up a feeling described by other parents in studies of parent-school communication with this comment: 'We feel we have to be on our best behaviour as well'. They are not alone in their experience of powerlessness to influence staff judgements and wider school policy. Researchers find that parents often feel infantilised in their contact with school staff. Crozier (2002) reports a parent saying: 'Sometimes when I go into school and they're talking to you, I feel intimidated because ... you feel as if you're the kid'. Walker and MacLure (2001), in their study of parents' evenings, note that even the parents who are teachers themselves feel powerless.

This need not be the case. Recent research on home-school communication, especially during the early years of school, has revealed examples of good practice where there is a deliberate attempt to minimise power differentials and create a genuine exchange of information (Whalley, 2001; Draper and Duffy, 2001; Hughes and Greenhough, 2006). Whilst Shelley's parents had lasting negative feelings about the early years schooling problem, we will see that the effect on Shelley herself was much less clear cut.

Shelley's positive approach to secondary school

Critiques have been made of 'infant determinism', the idea that experiences in early childhood set a path for later experiences and cannot be reversed (see Chapter 2). Shelley's story indicates that early experiences *can* be significantly reversed. When I met Shelley again at age twelve, during her second year at Forest Hill High School, she described herself in extremely positive ways. Whilst watching the video of her younger self, she commented on how she had changed: 'I just look bored then to what I am now in school. I'm just different. I've got loads of friends now and I'm good at my work'. Later, when I asked her specifically about the change from primary to secondary school, she said: 'I'm more happy'.

Twelve year old Shelley came across as co-operative and willing to talk. She appeared at ease. During the sequence of interviews that took place during year 8 of school, she showed a readiness to laugh. She spoke several times about her personal happiness in the context of secondary school. Her rationale for the selection of figures on the tree diagram that she considered to be most like her (Appendix 2) were based on a sense of herself as 'happy'. In her first interview she picked figures 13 and 15: 'that one and that one because they're both happy'. In her third interview seven months later, she picked number 10 and number 13 again because 'they look happy'. She explained her reason for the selection of the figure that she considered to be least like her, number 16, according to this same criterion: 'Because he doesn't look happy at all. Really grumpy'.

Two further self perceptions were of central importance to Shelley when she was interviewed at this time, and both are strongly related to her sense of herself as happy: she felt she had good friends, and she liked to be recognised as 'good'. When asked to produce self descriptors in response to my request to 'think of as many things about you as possible, any words that describe you as a person ... just try and bombard me...', Shelley said: 'Friendly, happy ... good'. Elaborating on these descriptors she said: I've just got loads of friends ... I'm always smiling ... And laughing. I can't stop laughing at school sometimes.'

It is possible that the emergence of the continuing value for goodness, expressed in association with being 'happy', during the series of year 8 interviews, may have been partly a legacy, though deeply implicit, of the disapproval engendered through her 'bad' behaviour when she started school. To myself as an observer, Shelley's transformation into a positive and self confident secondary school pupil was very marked. Of course I had not witnessed her gradual metamorphosis during the missing years in our acquaintance and especially the significant move into Forest Hill High.

Getting somewhere and doing something – Shelley in adolescence

Recent research focusing on the growing number of young people who are not in employment, education or training (NEETS) in the UK, has identified that many young people lack a sense of their own future. In Chapter 10 I discuss Liam, who, at seventeen years old, clearly fitted this pattern. But Shelley did not fit it at all. On the contrary, she was goal driven and seemed able to picture an adventurous and exciting future for herself. Her ambition was to pursue an acting career.

At the age of fifteen, towards the end of her years at secondary school (Forest Hill High School had no sixth form), Shelley spoke about her plans for the future:

JW: Have you got any plans for what you're going to do next?

S: I want to go to University.

JW: Do you?

S: Yes.

JW: What do you want to do?

S: I wanted to be a marine biologist but I don't anymore and I'm interested in acting so I don't know if I want to do that but I want to work with animals, so I don't know.

Shelley was definite about going to university. Given her multiple career interests and uncertainty about a specific course of study, this choice appeared to be more about going to university per se rather than as a means to a specific career. It was an interesting assertion, given that university entrance was far from the norm for Forest Hill pupils. Quite a high proportion of students from Forest Hill carry on to a local college of further education and some may then go on to university, but the proportion is very small. Whereas Martin (Chapter 5) at St Stephen's was surrounded by peers applying to university, a choice that was taken for granted by his teachers, parents and friends. Shelley's school reference group was not aspirational in this way. What was the source of her clearly articulated aspirations for higher education?

I teased this out more carefully when I met Shelley again at the age of seventeen. By then Tess and Brian had moved from the small town in which Shelley had been brought up to a rural location about twenty miles away. Shelley spent weekends and some week days living in her parents' new home but she stayed in the town overnight with her old next door neighbour, Maura, to attend the local 6th form college. I asked her what these changes meant for her and especially whether she missed living in town. She was clear that she missed some of her friends but was emphatic that 'I don't miss living round here'. I took this and the accompanying giggle to mean that she didn't think much of the part of town where she had been raised. I linked this disparaging view with the wishes to move away from the area altogether that became more evident in our conversation.

Two years later, during my conversation with seventeen year old Shelley, she was able to say more about her future goals. Having gained good GCSE results (General Certificate of Secondary Education) and being part way into a BTEC in Performing Arts (Business and Technology Education Council: vocational qualification with equivalence to A-levels) she was well on the road to achieving a university place to advance her wish to be an actress, with her eye on a particular degree course in London. Her rationale for higher education in the extract from the interview below stressed her wish to *do* something. She repeated this and I speculated that what appealed to her was the adventure and escape from the humdrum world of the small town she had lived in all her life. She used the term 'escapism' at a later point in the conversation, to describe her enjoyment of acting. Her earlier career aspiration to be a marine biologist, discussed when she was fifteen, which she linked to her interest in dolphins, was also a rather glamorous and escapist career choice. So it seemed that her wish to go into higher education was for adventure and for *doing* something. She gave an interesting answer to my question about the value of her school experience, again stressing her value for higher education. I asked: 'What does school do for people? What's the point of school?'

> S: Teaches them and you know, guides them, erm like a footpath, into higher education, guides them into that.
>
> JW: Did you see that as the main point?
>
> S: Yeah.
>
> JW: When did you decide this was a goal of yours?
>
> S: I've always wanted to. Thought about going to higher education cos I've always wanted to *do* something.

Simons *et al* use the term 'future time perspective' (FTP) to describe 'the present anticipation of future goals' (2004:122). McInerney *et al* (2004), who also discuss FTP, found that motivated pupils who were doing well at school had a clear rationale for school and could present the pathway they would take on leaving. Shelley gave a clear illustration of FTP, and I was curious to find out why. Was she motivated by the desire to stand out from the majority of her peer group, who mainly held lower aspirations regarding university entrance? I was intrigued to learn more from Shelley about the kinds of social comparisons she made with her immediate peer group during her secondary school career, especially regarding academic aspirations. I was aware of social class comparisons buried within statements made by her parents during the early phase of the study. Tess's criticisms of the parents who let their children play in the streets and Brian's description of Francoise's family as 'rough, very rough', were forms of social 'othering'. I wondered to what extent the family shared a strong agenda for moving up the social class ladder. I asked Shelley about her parents' aspirations for her:

> JW: What do your Mum and Dad want for you when they think about your future?
>
> S: For me to do what I want to do. For me to do well and get where I want to be. Not mess round.

> JW: What would that be for them – messing around?
>
> S: Not taking my career seriously and just dropping out of college and university.

I prompted Shelley to make more explicit comparisons with others, especially those who might be regarded as her 'outgroup'. I wanted to know what kind of future these people would have, how different their futures would be to Shelley's and whether she was aware of this difference. The nearest we got to this was her identification of 'people who throw pencils', a remark made in response to a question about the downside of school: 'People throwing pencils in class. Really really annoying [giggles]. It didn't get them anywhere'.

Her comment was clearly linked to her own aspirations to 'get somewhere'. Values for getting to 'where I want to be', having clear future goals, and taking a career seriously emerged as key personal goals, goals she shared with her parents. For example when I asked her about her reasons for choosing to go to college, whereas some of her friends had not, she explained this was so she could get 'more qualifications'. And the point of this? 'Do more stuff. Get where I want to be. You need more qualifications to do the things you want to do'.

When I asked about the labels she and her friends used to describe other groups at school, Shelley told me more about her outgroup, the 'others' in her life. This was not easy and I found I was putting words in her mouth by mentioning some youth sub culture labels that currently prevail, such as 'Goths', 'Emos' and 'Chavs'. Shelley giggled and refused to be drawn on this. However when I asked her about teachers' perceptions of groups in school and how her own friendship group would be categorised, she instantly produced the adjectives 'good' and 'helpful' to characterise her own group.

> JW: As distinct from? How might they [the teachers] describe other groups in school?
>
> S: Noisy, not bothered with their work.

'Working' and 'not working' seemed to be two important poles for Shelley of positioning within school. When imagining how some of her peers might see her, Shelley relied on the idea of hard work.

> JW: What would somebody at school who didn't like you very much say about you?

S: They'd probably call me a swot.

During this final interview I asked Shelley a question about her personal change. Her answer suggested that she now had goals whereas she didn't before.

JW: What things about you changed? About you yourself?

S: A lot of things have changed. [Pause] Like what I've been wanting to do with my life and stuff.

She seemed to be implying not to so much that her specific aspirations had changed but that she had become aspirational. So a strong feature of the way Shelley presented herself to me at age seventeen was as a person who had clear goals and was definitely on the way to achieving them.

The nature of Shelley's goals is worth discussing too, as her enthusiasm for acting was interesting in relation to her construction of self. She clearly saw the ability to get up on stage and perform, as she had done several times at school, as an important aspect of her self-image. Significantly, she identified this ability as something that marked a dramatic change from the young Shelley, whom she perceived, retrospectively, to have been 'shy'. She spoke about this transformation in her identity at fifteen, when asked about her choice of Performing Arts as a GCSE subject: this, she explained, was 'a recent thing, I used to be really shy'.

Tracking this transformation back through the course of the study it is interesting to note the data I collected from Shelley's first year at Bridge View primary about her first public performance. Tess had told me about a Mother's Day event in which Shelley had been required to sing songs and perform accompanying actions on stage to an audience of parents. She had told me about this as an illustration of how 'lost' Shelley was during the first year of school: 'Shelley looked, well, frightened, like she didn't dare move ... Shelley just sat there looking worried'.

So Shelley found her gradual development of an enjoyment of performing to be quite a significant change. Here she is at fifteen, saying a little more about how this came about, communicating a sense of surprise and pleasure at the status implied in being selected for the 'main' part:

When I was doing my first production ... I was the main character because I only wanted a small part in the play and then I just got the main part and I just liked doing acting and stuff. I was just like filling in for people who weren't there and I got the main part.

During her interview at age seventeen Shelley said more about her motivation to act and how she had been especially impressed with the acting talents of an older year 10 pupil, emphasising again her satisfaction in setting herself a goal and then achieving it:

I was in the chorus at first. I saw one of the main characters and I thought 'I can do that' and I did. I got the main part. She was really good. She inspired me. I thought 'I just want to try that'.

Shelley emerged from these last interviews as an aspirational young woman on an upward trajectory based on implicit goals for social mobility and adventure and an explicit vocation for acting.

Conclusions

My story of Shelley illustrates several features of the business of self making. Firstly it underlines the influence of the socio-cultural context by revealing a discontinuity between the two major contexts of home and school. The story of Shelley's transition to primary school serves to remind us that people can appear to be different people in different contexts. This has an impact on the development of self, but only at the point that young people themselves become aware of these multiple selves, which is usually not until adolescence. Secondly, her story is a salutary tale of parent/teacher conflict. It relates to the literature on the need for good relations between home and school, so these major contexts can be mutually reinforcing. Thirdly, her story challenges theories of infant determinism, since the biggest impact of the home-school conflict was probably on Shelley's parents rather on herself, with Shelley constructing a 'happy' identity during her secondary school career. Finally, in the last phase of the study Shelley illustrates the purposeful trajectory of a young person who has managed to construct a future self.

8

Simon's story: fateful moments as a prompt for the story of self

Introduction

The main plot in my telling of Simon's story concerns his relationships with peers. His fear of being bullied emerged during his primary school years and the transition to secondary school. They became a reality when Simon was violently attacked near his home one night, aged fifteen, by a large gang of boys. This event significantly and negatively affected his subsequent school career. In this Chapter I reflect on how a critical incident such as this can become a central feature in a person's story of self. Indeed, it can become a prompt for the act of telling such a story. Simon's strategy for strengthening his self following this incident relied on literally strengthening his body through physical exercise and sport, and on seizing the opportunity given by professional therapeutic support to find the words to voice his ideas about self.

I first met Simon during his pre-school year when he was four, and this is where my story begins. I also met the people who formed his social world: Kath (his mother), Paul (his father), Garry (older brother), Laura (baby sister), the staff who worked in his pre-school and some of his friends there. I commence by examining his social relationships during the first phase of the study, as I began to get to know him. As my reading of Simon's development of self foregrounds his peer relationships, I have more to say about this aspect of his overall social world than his relationship with parents, siblings or staff, although these other relationships are implicated in the patterns of his peer relationships. The questions that informed my initial attempts to get to know Simon were those that are central to this book. I wanted to see to what extent a sense of self emerged during the time when Simon's world was expanding socially to include other significant people besides his immediate family.

'Social understanding' in the nursery

Some vignettes of four year old Simon at play and in interaction with his peer set the scene. They are based on the observational notes and video footage I made whilst he was at Brompton nursery in the summer term before he started at Brompton primary school, and also during his early days of the new school. The nursery was brand new: 'purpose built', the manager recently appointed and full of enthusiasm, proudly displaying the latest state-of the art resources she had ordered. There was a spacious and well equipped outdoor area adjoining the primary school. A small person could just about see the school buildings over the wall at the back.

The pedagogic principles of this nursery were based entirely on unstructured play. The only structured event was that each child spent a brief period each day seated at a table for milk and fruit. This phase of the study pre-dates the advent of the UK National Curriculum Foundation Stage for 3-6 year olds and there was very little in the way of staff-directed activity. The children were entirely free to choose from the many activities and resources permanently available. My observations of Simon, and the other children, showed that this often made for a pattern of unfocused wandering, interspersed with focused activity. Because the children had so much scope for making choices about activities, toys and materials as well as social choices about which people to be with, this was a rich site for observing children's implicit and explicit choices and preferences. A more teacher-directed environment reveals less about the child's own preferences.

> Simon is playing in the sand. Others are there too but he is not interacting with them. He is completely absorbed in his play with the sand and with the various coloured plastic sand tools. He puts the tools down and moves off to the car mat, an aerial diagram of roads and garages. He moves toy cars about on this. I haven't heard him speak yet. Later in the morning I observe

Simon again. He is now playing a chasing game with two other boys in the outdoor play area. These are David (another child in my study) and Owen. David goes to collect a ball and the game turns to football. (Notes from video recording, Brompton nursery, June visit 8)

Simon is back at the sand. Again he is absorbed and careful with the materials. Later I watch him as he plays with the construction toys, seated at a table with David and Owen. I notice that Simon's play is very purposeful. He is playing with a Brio™ construction kit, selecting all the blue pegs from a basket and hammering them into the right slots in three different lengths of wood. He appears to be guided by a clear sense of what he is trying to achieve. He sets out all the green pegs he can find in a line. David copies his plan. David and Simon are close together. They both seem intensely involved in the activity and it looks as if their mutual absorption is motivating them. They work in silence. (Notes from video recording, Brompton nursery, July visit 12)

This is what the observers of young children's play call 'playing along-side', or 'parallel play'. It is the foundation for social forms of play (Parten, 1932; Broadhead, 2004), said to typify the play behaviour of young children under the age of four (Faulkner, 1995; Sylva *et al*, 1980). Whilst many researchers of young children's play are interested in how such activities influence the young child's cognitive development, I was especially interested in the socio-emotional aspects of this encounter. This unspoken engagement appeared, from my perspective, to be a good way of building up a comfortable familiarity, providing emotional security in the busy social world of the nursery.

Most of the children are outside enjoying the fine weather. Simon is playing with David and Owen on a go-cart. Simon is seated in it and is making it go very fast. He looks as if he is enjoying himself. Owen moves away and Simon continues the activity with David. He lets David push him. Then, without a word spoken between them, he and David change places so that Simon is now pushing David. Then Simon moves off on his own to find another vehicle and then another. Next he goes into the caterpillar tunnel and remains hidden there for a few minutes. He perhaps needs this little break from the bustle. (Notes from video recording, Brompton nursery, July visit 13)

Reflecting on this brief episode, especially the quality of the relation-ship between the playmates, I believe it is the non verbal co-operation that is most striking. Broadhead's observations of play reveal 'a kind of telepathy' young children sometimes display when they play co-operatively together with a very minimal, or non-existent, use of language (Broadhead, 2004:9). Observers of young children's play suggest that co-operative play begins to emerge when children are over three years old (Green, 2002). So Simon and David are not untypical. Broadhead presents levels of social co-operation in young children's play as the 'social play continuum'. This brief action by the two boys of swapping positions as pusher and driver of the car belongs to the rather simple end of this continuum, with verbally negotiated role playing at the more advanced end. Nevertheless it is interesting to analyse further. Their behaviour might mean that they have taken on board the turn-taking 'rules' which are a strong feature of the pedagogy for this age group, the request to 'share' being frequently voiced by the nursery staff. It may also be that the two boys intuitively recognise a value for fairness in their access to the go-cart, entailing some understanding of one another's feelings and the likelihood of disappointment if they don't get a turn. This is a rudimentary form of 'social understanding', the concept presented by Dunn (1988), discussed in Chapter 3, which provides the building blocks for children's capacity to empathise. Hartup (1992) claims that social behaviour in the pre-school years is more competent, reciprocal and complementary with a stable friend, than with an unstable one. My strong impression was that this example of self directed turn taking would have been less likely to take place between peers who were unfamiliar with each other, and was a product of the bond between Simon and David that was becoming established through parallel play. It entailed some recognition of the feelings of the other.

The 'rest' that Simon took, hidden from his peers in the caterpillar tunnel, is also worth noting, in light of similar incidents of 'hiding' observed later on when Simon started in the Reception class of formal school. I interpreted these incidents as a way for Simon to gain some temporary respite from the noise and bustle of the classroom and playground and they alerted me to his need for quiet, which remained a consistent feature of his personality.

As I began to collect together more observational snapshots of Simon interacting with peers and as I spoke with staff and parents, and sometimes with Simon himself, certain of my impressions were reaffirmed. I identified significant themes which seemed to have a bearing on his social relationships, the beginnings of social understanding and the early emergence of self.

Firstly, he seemed quiet compared with many of the other children and seldom smiled. Sue Hudson, the nursery manager, described him as a 'rather solemn child', but he did not look ill at ease in the nursery. I interpreted his quietness as being due to his absorption in the play materials rather than as shyness or insecurity within the social setting of the nursery.

Secondly, his peer group was nearly always exclusively male. His choices about playmates were compounded by his choices of activity, which were on the whole rather gender stereotypical. Broadhead (2004) points to the overlap in children's attraction to players and play situations as the pragmatic source of social peer groups. Simon seemed to have a particular liking for toy cars (miniature and child-sized), a preference superseded during adolescence by his interest in real cars, shared with his father. I also noted which toys and activities he did not use: the rack of dressing-up clothes, the dolls, domestic 'kitchen' equipment, and the book area.

When questioned about his preferred activities Simon himself said: 'outside, play-dough, cars, garage, jigsaws'. He answered this question quickly and easily, his answers consistent with my observations. I gained the impression that this was a child who knew what he liked doing, who had a feeling of agency. The SEAL recommendations (social and emotional aspects of learning) enshrined in the government's 2005 *Excellence and Enjoyment* (DfES, 2005) suggest that a child within the Foundation Stage (age 3-5) should be able to articulate the things they like doing and that such a capacity is important in establishing the self.

The gendered nature of Simon's choice of playmates was typical for this age group (Schaffer, 1996; Thorne, 1993). When asked about the people he liked to play with, he could quickly produce a list of names, all male: 'Ryan, Owen, David, Michael and Sam'. Most, but not all, of those listed had been observed playing with Simon. He did not identify a special friend and was not observed to have an exclusive 'best friend' relationship, but this would be unusual at preschool age (Hartup, 1992). Simon's easy recognition and identification of playmates confirmed his secure group membership within the nursery.

111

Thirdly, the quality of Simon's peer relationships was noteworthy. He was certainly capable of playing alongside other children and I witnessed many instances of parallel play, and some examples of co-operative play, which suggested a comfortable familiarity with specific peers such as David. This is the bedrock of peer friendship which develops in a more pronounced way when verbal communication comes into play. He was not usually the centre of the group, a role taken by his friend David, who played the clown and made others laugh. David and Owen were more likely than Simon to initiate a change of activity with a confident verbal suggestion: 'Let's go out now'. Simon would generally either follow their lead or silently and independently undertake a new activity of his own choosing.

Overall, my observations of Simon during this period confirmed my original impression that, though quiet and sometimes happy to play on his own, he was well ensconced in his peer group. This augured well for an unproblematic transition into the new social context of Brompton primary school.

Adapting to school

Brompton school was already familiar to Simon as it was near the nursery and because his older brother Garry was already there and Simon regularly went along to fetch him. In addition Simon had twice visited the Reception class with the other nursery children as part of the school's transition policy. There was a carefully phased start at this school so that, for the first few weeks, he only attended in the morning, rather than the whole day, in a small group of children, the whole class only coming together for a full day after the first Half Term holiday (the induction strategy which operated in the other primary schools in this study). For all these reasons the commencement of school might have been less traumatic than for children who come to a totally unfamiliar school setting. Nevertheless, he was in an unfamiliar classroom with unfamiliar adults and some unfamiliar fellow pupils. Importantly, expectations about school work and 'proper' pupil behaviour are present in subtle forms in the Reception classroom (Brooker, 2002; Maclure and Jones, 2009). I wondered how he would adapt. In particular I wondered how this significant set of new experiences would influence the development of his sense of self.

> As I enter the Reception class Simon is rolling play dough with a look of intense concentration. Simon moves off and wanders about the classroom. He goes into the home corner and squats down out of sight in a corner and I wonder whether he is giving himself time out. He goes over to the bead table, then to the water play area and finally returns to the play dough where he re-engages in his previous activity. He cuts out long slivers of dough and slices them carefully into tiny rolls, with impressive dexterity. (Notes from video recording, Brompton primary school, September, visit 1)

I was interested in the way Simon flitted from one activity to another. This 'butterfly' behaviour was an aspect of the transition to school that particularly struck me in my observation of all ten children when they started in their school classes (see Shelley's story). Some of the children seemed rather more focused on the materials and physical attributes of the classroom than on the other children within it. Simon seemed to be in this category during the initial few weeks when the new materials were unfamiliar to him, and he engaged in an exploration of his environment. It seems likely that children who have fewer possessions at home are more likely to be drawn to the physical resources of the classroom and this may have been the case for Simon. However, as the environment became more familiar, he homed in on his fellow pupils, showing more awareness of them through imitation, and building on the co-operation skills I had observed in his preschool.

> Simon's class are taken into the school hall for a PE lesson. Simon smiles as he hops up and down. A lot of the children are laughing and he joins in. I realise he is the tallest of the ten children in the hall. When Mrs Rogers [classroom assistant] bangs a tambourine, he claps his hands over his ears and looks startled, then smiles when he realises others are smiling and laughing. He concentrates on his marching and looks absorbed and happy. Later I observe him doing jigsaws. He is playing alongside another boy. They are involved in tacit turn taking as they take the jigsaw pieces out of the box. (Notes from video recording, Brompton primary school, September, visit 6)

During the course of the year Simon consolidated his existing association with David and formed a new friendship with Michael. When asked to nominate his friends, towards the end of the Reception class year, he produced these names quickly but did not list any others. His choice was confirmed by his Reception class teacher, Mrs Long. By the end of this year he had formed positive and stable peer relationships in school. Simon was not part of a culture of mutual invitations to the home so there was no overlap between his peer relationships in school and at home, where his playmates were his older brother Garry and younger sister Laura.

Despite this reasonably positive start to his school career, several related features of his transition to the Reception class seem significant to his overall coping and development of self, especially where they reveal the seeds of later developments. There were signs that he found it was more stressful than I had anticipated. Kath, Simon's mother, made a brief record of his initial response to school in the notebook I had provided for this purpose. She recorded that he 'becomes very quiet' when he goes into the classroom. She also noted; 'Simon has been getting upset at dinner times. He does not like eating his dinner in the junior hall. It seems it is too overpowering for him'.

Her sense that certain aspects of school were 'too overpowering' was echoed by the Reception class teacher, who said 'I think he's awed by the whole thing sometimes'.

Both Kath and Mrs Long made similar comments that emphasised Simon's 'quietness', reinforcing what I had observed in pre-school. Kath's notes recorded that he was 'quiet at first with his teacher'. When Mrs Long gave me her impressions of Simon, she said that she did not feel she had a very good relationship with him: 'He's a bubbly little boy but he's also quiet. He doesn't respond well to me. He might respond better to a quieter teacher'. When I interviewed Mrs Long later, in year 1 (as she continued to be Simon's class teacher), Simon's avoidance of her had become more entrenched: 'I think he is quite terrified of me actually'. She contrasted him with his more gregarious brother, Garry, whom she had also taught, and with his friend David, saying:

> To be perfectly honest, Simon never, never actually, you know, stuck out at all, of all the children. Very quiet. Pally with David. David will take the lead more than Simon. He'll sort of say 'This is what's happening' and Simon will follow. No, he doesn't really stick out. He just sort of merged into everybody else.

Although I acknowledge the dilemma faced by teachers in attending to the needs of quiet children alongside the demands of the more vociferous (Collins, 1996), I was unsettled by Mrs Long's lack of attention to Simon, now that I had his wellbeing at heart. There was clearly some consensus about his quietness and this trait seems to have remained quite consistent. It was confirmed by Simon himself at a later stage of the study. It also related to his mother's frequent use of the term 'sensitive' to describe him, and her perception that, 'if anybody shouts at him he's upset'.

Social relationships in the early years of school

During the early phase of the study there was no expectation that children would have the ability to articulate descriptions of self. I expected statements about self to be limited to the concrete aspects of their lives, such as who they played with, which people were in their family, what toys and activities they preferred. However, at the end of their second year of formal school I tried to tease out their ideas about how they had changed during the time they had been at school. This was my exchange with Simon:

> JW: Let's think about how you have changed during the time you have been at school. Do you think you have changed?
>
> S: Yes. When it's sunny I smile and when it's a bit sunny I like it. When it's cloudy I like it.
>
> JW: Hmm [Quiet laugh]. Have you become slightly different as you've got older?
>
> S: Yes.
>
> JW: In what ways
>
> S: [Long pause] Don't know.
>
> JW: You've grown haven't you? You've got taller. Are there any things that you can do now?
>
> S: I can ride my bike. I can paint. I can do handstands, cartwheels, run.

Simon's initial, rather unpredictable weather-related comments are hard to read. He perhaps intuited that I was interested in his feelings. Perhaps he was genuinely influenced by the weather on that day and its changeability. The conversation certainly illustrates the unpredictability and difficulty of interpretation in analysing conversations with young children and shows how questioning can often be rather laboured and unproductive. With prompting, Simon was able to think about the development of specific skills: things he could do now that he couldn't do before. Harter (1999:36) points out that when children of this age look back on their younger selves and reflect on changes, they tend to emphasise their performance and skills. Suls and Sanders (1982) suggest that this emphasis in self descriptions reflects children's satisfaction with the rapid skills development that characterises this phase, a view that is reflected in Simon's final, prompted, statement.

What did Simon himself think about his social relationships during the early years of school? His own nomination of 'friends' during pre-school, Reception class and year 1 are depicted in Table 1, the names presented in the order they were mentioned. Simon's nominations were consistent with my observations and with comments by the teachers and his mother about his peer preferences. He also explained, on all these three occasions, that he played at home with his siblings, his older brother Garry, baby sister Laura and, later, in year 1 conversation, his new baby brother Rory, talking with obvious pleasure and pride about these family relationships.

Table 1. Simon's nominations for friends in pre-school/school (ages 4 – 6)

Pre-school (age 3- 4)	Reception (age 4 – 5)	Year 1 (age 5- 6)
Owen, Robert, Nathan, David	David and Michael	Michael and David. Also plays with Tom, Lee, Jamie and Matt.

The choices over the three years confirm the pattern of same-sex play-mates, a pattern that also relates to his mother's perception that his interests are in 'lad's things': 'Footballing, bicycle, the tools in the garage. He goes there with his Dad'.

Mrs Long remarked that Simon 'doesn't go out of his peer group. He stays very much with the same small group of boys'. Whilst this pattern might perhaps indicate a lack of social risk-taking, it confirmed that Simon had developed stable friendships. This was significant in two ways that concerned his self development. Firstly, the feeling of belonging contributes to wellbeing (Smith, 1986; Langsted, 1994; Fabian, 2002; Warin and Muldoon 2009). Secondly, the development of exclusive friendships over time creates the social context for the development of self awareness (Youniss, 1980).

I have chosen to focus on Simon's peer relationships as a major feature in his story of self. The pattern of peer relationships is clearly related to his relationships with adults and to the overall experience of being at school. Academic status impacts on children's sense of self and the ways they are perceived by peers, which in turn influences and is further influenced by how they come to see themselves. During the early part of school, and particularly as the requirements of the national curriculum begin to be experienced, a child will be aware of the pressures to succeed academically. When Mrs Long filled in the 'cognitive competence' items for the PSPCSA scale devised by Harter and Pike (1983), she gave Simon low scores. She also gave a verbal account of his difficulties in reading: 'He struggles, poor lad. He does struggle with reading and numbers. You have to keep repeating things'. By the end of year 1, Kath was also aware of these problems and was clearly anxious about this area of Simon's school life: 'We think he may be dyslexic. We are worried about his lack of concentration. He keeps forgetting little words that he is supposed to have learned'. Given his difficulties, it was perhaps easier for Simon to avoid Mrs Long by seeking company in his peer group who tended to remain at a distance from their teacher.

During his second year of school a new feature of his peer relationships emerged. Both Mrs Long and Kath commented that Simon had been drawn into playground fights, influenced by the boisterous and often aggressive play of his group of friends. When discussing Simon's peer relations with Mrs Long, I asked about children he might avoid or dislike. Her response revealed his lack of assertiveness with certain 'dominant' pupils:

> I'd say Nathan and Chandra because they're really really dominant characters, and although he's easily, well quite easily led, I don't think he likes being bossed around, but he wouldn't feel confident enough to tell Nathan to go away or to stop bullying him and I don't think he would be able to do that with Chandra either.

Kath voiced fears about Simon being 'picked on' in year 1 by his peers and, interestingly, speculated about his own contribution to peer conflicts: 'I wondered if he was being picked on but it may be six of one and half a dozen of the other'. Later in the same interview she said:

> He's a very sensitive boy. He says 'I don't like fighting'... I know what he's going through. I was sensitive myself. I was never a fighter. He got a bit un-

settled at dinner times – with Michael, David and him. This is where some hitting was going on'.

It emerged from the data that Simon did not feel confident about responding to more assertive peers, especially where this took physical form, yet various types and degrees of physical fighting, from 'play fights' to more serious conflicts, were a significant part of the culture of his male peer group. He did not show the same enjoyment of boisterous playground activities that characterised the play behaviour of some of the other children in the sample.

By the end of this phase of the study I concluded that Simon had gained membership of the dominant male peer group in his class and this gave him a combination of emotional security and discomfort over the aggressive aspects of male behaviour. His academic performance was causing his parents and staff some concern, though not necessarily Simon himself. When I pictured Simon in the intervening period of time, I saw him as a quiet, sensitive boy, well integrated into a small stable peer group which provided him with the context for the ongoing development of his awareness of self and others.

Reflections on the move to secondary school

When I decided to meet with the nine young people in year 8 of school, at age twelve/thirteen, a key intention was to find out how they had experienced the transition to secondary school. How far had it stirred up concerns about self?

Re-establishing contact with Simon seven years after the first phase of the study was relatively easy, as his family had remained at the same address. Kath had been particularly co-operative during the early phase of the study and seemed genuinely pleased to be contacted again. As the study progressed I became aware that she believed that Simon's participation was 'good for him', recognising that this opportunity might have a therapeutic value. I was less certain that Simon himself would be prepared to continue his involvement. But he, too, seemed willing to participate further. When I visited Simon for the first of the sequence of three interviews I held at this age, my main aim was to access self beliefs and reflections about the transition to secondary school.

Transitions from one phase of life to another provide fertile ground for the construction of identity. As a person's social group changes, and they move from a familiar set of social relationships with their peers and authority figures into another set of relationships, their thoughts about self are likely to be provoked and they will wonder how they are coming across (see discussion in Chapter 4). Strong underlying emotions characterise transitional phases, such as the desire to find friends and to 'belong', and fears about social rejection and isolation. Consequently 'the ongoing story of self' (Giddens, 1991) will be a more active project than at other times. A number of educational researchers have explored school transitions, particularly the major transition from primary to secondary school, to see how children's self perceptions are created and re-created during this time and what changes in self emerge. Measor and Woods (1984), Lucey and Reay (2000) and Warin and Muldoon (2009) all examine how existing beliefs about identity are disrupted at such times, producing anxieties and stimulating self consciousness.

As a way of re-acquainting ourselves, one of the first activities after the long gap was to make a timeline together of key incidents that had occurred since we last had contact seven years before (see Chapter 5). Simon's timeline depicted an uneventful life in which the most memorable moments had been the arrival of Grandma to live in his immediate neighbourhood, a trip to see Manchester United play football, a running race at primary school where he beat the fastest teacher, and two quite dramatic physical accidents: a minor electrocution and a fall from a tree from which he received a deep cut to his leg. The creation of the timeline also gave me the opportunity to see whether the move to his secondary school (St Mary's, a large Catholic comprehensive near his home) was mentioned as a key event. It wasn't.

However, he spoke about the anxieties he had experienced during this significant change later when he was more relaxed. He discussed the change from feeling like a big fish in a small pond in primary school to the experience of starting at the bottom again: 'You're like top and then when you go into high school you're bottom again'. He spoke of the greater 'strictness' of teachers: 'Some are proper strict and you want to talk but you can't cause they're like rrrr, they go mad ... Just don't talk, just sit quiet and just do what teacher tells you'. He also identified the problem of the size of the new school and all the classrooms, and echoed the research of others who have found concerns about getting lost: 'more rooms to remember cause at Primary School you only used to be in one room, now it's just like all everywhere'. The main anxieties he spoke of conform to the patterns that are found in other research on this transition (see above).

Kath mentioned twice that Simon had 'some problems' during the transition into St Mary's but that he had 'settled'. Simon seemed to collude with this view but neither of them were explicit about the nature of the 'problems' However, as the conversation continued, it became apparent that these were linked to self perceptions about peer relations that had begun to emerge in his early primary school career. His strongest anxieties about transition were about the possibility of his being pushed around by bigger people and getting implicated in fights: 'When I started there I was proper all scared and stuff about all the big people pushing you about and stuff but now I'm alright with it'. He told me:

> Sometimes I see all these big gangs and stuff and it makes me just all go 'oh no here we go, something's going to happen and all this'. Sometimes I'm like that with my friends cause they like try to start fights and I'm going 'no I'm not going to do that' and all this and they're like 'ohhh'.

Statements about these fears echoed some of the ambivalence about his male peer relationships that had been discernible in the early phase of the research. He appeared to feel alienated and uncomfortable with 'big gangs', which raised the possibility of fighting, and he wanted to distance himself from them.

When I met Kath again after the seven year break she revealed some significant information about Simon's primary school career. During the later primary school years, he had started to run off on his way to school and refused to go into school. At this, time she reported, he was 'really fed up' with school and especially with 'being bullied'. Simon confirmed this issue of bullying, describing an incident that occurred in year 5, when he was ten, in which he was not able to perform his usual strategy: 'to walk away':

> I used to get bullied mainly most of the time. One time I was getting annoyed, getting picked on all the time, so I was just walking away and this lad started pushing me in the back so I bust all his eye there and this book dude came

out. He was overweight and stuff. So I just punched him and he fell on the floor and then I never got done basically cause they started it.

Simon seemed to tell his story as a way of explaining his hostility to school and vindicating his feeling of being bullied. The account did not appear to be motivated by guilt over his own violent actions, nor by pride or bravado. He seemed to be saying that the bullying he experienced must have been extreme in order to provoke him to this degree. He did not offer a commentary on the incident, and did not seem reflect on it to produce any statements about self.

Construction of self at age twelve

The major aim of the three meetings with the children during their second year in secondary school (aged twelve/thirteen) was to test out how far they were constructing a continuous story of self. I tried out several strategies for stimulating self beliefs: discussion of school reports, preferred photos and the use of the figurative 'tree of life' (Appendix 2). The full range is described in detail in Chapter 5. I focused especially on two key lines of discussion: What has changed about you? What has remained the same? Harter (1999) claims that children begin to employ trait labels that focus on abilities and interpersonal characteristics during middle to late childhood. At this stage they make more abstract generalisations about self that incorporate several behaviours and they recognise that characteristics are repeated over time. They are less likely to produce the concrete self descriptions of younger children, based on skills, physical attributes and possessions. When asked to reflect back and make comparisons with themselves when they were younger, stimulated by watching video extracts of their younger selves, most children typified this pattern.

Simon seemed to find it harder than some of the other children to produce the abstract terms required to construct a story of self. Some of his responses to my attempts showed him creating literal and concrete representations of self more akin to how younger children respond. For example his responses to the request to identify two comparison figures on the 'tree of life' seemed to stimulate his interest in tree climbing rather than his interest in making statements about his self. So when he was asked to justify his selection of the figure, he said: 'Cause I've climbed like big trees, like, you know, at Ellington Park, and I climb up them sometimes'.

121

When I asked Simon to select three significant others in his life and try to imagine their perceptions of him by putting himself in their shoes, he again produced concrete descriptions which emphasise what he believed he was 'good at' and what he *did*, the activities he engaged in. So, for example, when thinking about how his friend Chris would see him, he said: 'He'd probably say I'm good at football'. His Uncle Wayne would say 'That I eat a lot'. His Grandma: 'That I help with the shopping, help tidy up a bit. I kind of hoover and stuff'. When I asked him 'to tell me as many things as possible about you', Simon managed to produce a list of self descriptors (see Chapter 5 for a discussion of this research tactic) but again these were focused on the practical and the concrete.

> Boy, 'like climbing, running, fixing things, making things, playing on computers, going out playing pool with my mates and stuff in arcades, errr, watching DVD's buying loads of things (then with prompting). Helpful, I lend people stuff, sometimes I argue with my Mum or my Dad or my brother (more prompting). I'm quite kind with other people.

One abstract trait label Simon acknowledged to be accurate was the term 'quiet'. He showed us his school reports from the first two years of secondary school. Asked whether the teachers had got it right, he agreed with the qualities they had identified: 'Yes my running and I am quite quiet'. Taken together, the various attempts to prompt self statements revealed Simon's difficulties in doing so. How far does this mean he was lacking in self awareness? Does it mean he was emotionally illiterate?

Clearly, emotional literacy is related to cognitive and linguistic abilities. Goleman (1996), for example, notes a link between IQ and emotional intelligence. We have seen that Simon's Reception class and year 1 teacher, Mrs Long, rated Simon's cognitive abilities as low, and that literacy problems were also identified in year 1. Kath told us that her worries about Simon's learning problems in his early primary career had led to an assessment for dyslexia. By the time he started secondary school Simon had a statement of special educational needs and was receiving learning support.

Simon found it hard to respond to the abstract nature of the questions designed to prompt self statements. Other children provided fuller and more nuanced statements about how they saw themselves, and reflections on how they had changed. What does this comparison mean for Simon and what does it mean for conclusions about the emergence of self through the school career? To describe Simon as lacking in emotional literacy may say as much about a lack of opportunities in his life for developing the vocabulary and values associated with this term as about his cognitive abilities. It may mean that, in contrast to Martin, for example, whose family culture promoted 'identity capital', Simon had had little occasion for the telling of self. Until, that is, a particular event or 'fateful moment' in his life, prompted both the need and the opportunity to create a more coherent story of self than he had created before. It is this to which I now turn.

A fateful moment in the construction of self

At the start of this Chapter I briefly introduced the topic of Simon's experience of being aggressively assaulted by a large gang of boys one night near his home, when he was fifteen and in year 9 of school. A physical attack on the person has an effect on the construction of self. Indeed, it is likely to be experienced to a certain extent as an attack on the self. In Simon's case the incident seems especially poignant, given the gradual build-up of his fears about bullying and his history of a rather ambivalent response to aggression within his all-male peer group.

The first time I heard about the attack was the very day after it had taken place. The timing of the incident coincided with contacting the children as they came to the end of their third year in secondary school, aged fourteen/fifteen. I rang Simon's family and his Dad, Paul, answered the phone. He told me at once that Simon had been 'beaten up' the night before: 'Fifteen lads started on him'. The family were shaken and preoccupied with their involvement with the police. Paul advised me to wait a while before contacting Simon for further meetings. When I eventually contacted the family again Kath gave me her account. Simon had been walking home at 1.00am and a gang of about fifteen lads of his own age or older had attacked him. Some were known to him, some attended his school, and some were strangers. The attack took place at the end of the summer term. Simon did not return to St Mary's that term and then, after the six week vacation, found it too daunting to go back into school, so he did not start year 10, and returned eventually in the summer term of year 11 for the run up to GCSEs, having missed a good eighteen months of school.

Giddens' (1991) account of the 'reflexive project of the self', touched on in Chapter 3, is relevant here. Giddens recognises the significance of critical incidents, or 'fateful moments' to use his preferred term, in the telling of self. These are times 'when events come together in such a way that an individual stands, as it were, at a crossroads in his existence' (p113). Giddens typifies such moments in terms of some familiar key life decisions such as getting married, starting a new business, taking exams. But he also says 'It often happens that fateful moments occur because of events that impinge upon an individual's life willy-nilly... They are phases at which things are wrenched out of joint, where a given state of affairs is suddenly altered by a few key events' (p113). Henderson *et al* (2007), in their study of the biographies of young people 'inventing adulthoods', have used Giddens' ideas to reveal a wide range of key events including those that were within the control of the young people such as changing schools, exams, 'coming out', and others that were entirely beyond their control such as bereavement, family disruption and violence. I now explore Simon's account of the attack specifically to see how far it matches Giddens' description of a fateful moment.

Simon's own account of the attack was yielded up in piecemeal fashion during the conversation we had together when he was seventeen. I began by asking him to 'catch me up with some of things that have happened since we last met'. He instantly plunged in. 'Did you know I got attacked?' However, he then moved on quickly to tell me about his recent job at Sampson Motors and his new-found interest in attending a local gym. Later, when I brought up the subject again:

> S: It's all sorted now. Finished.
>
> JW: It sounds like you don't want to talk about it.
>
> S: I never talk about it.

Later Simon mentioned an old friend of his who was in a Young Offenders Unit and this gave me a cue to ask about the fate of his attackers. Again he seemed anxious to avoid opening up this topic: 'I knew four or five of them through school, but it's all sorted now. Police have sorted it all out'.

It was in the context of a discussion about the role of schools in preventing bullying that Simon let go of his reserve. His frankness at this point seemed to be stimulated by anger with the attackers, people who 'batter' others, inside and outside school:

> When you're walking around [school] people are getting battered. It's not on. Like them that did me, said 'Oh we were just doing it for a laugh' but I nearly came out of it blind in one eye. I've still got a gap there in me chest [indicates]. They kicked me and punched me. Bit of a black eye as well. All sorts ... I'm so wary now of what's happening. After it happened I was just sleeping all the time. Just staying in bed. Watching telly. I had to build it up gradually. Like, first time I went into town after I got attacked I was really panicking. Breathing rate went up. Heart rate had gone up. Everything really. Sweating was constant.

It is interesting, and consistent with his familiar emphasis on the physical aspects of self, that Simon describes his bodily response to the experience of the fears engendered by the attack. He also, though, introduces a key self statement of a more abstract nature, about how the incident has changed him: 'I'm so wary now'.

'Strengthening' the self

Giddens identifies a further aspect of 'fateful moments', suggesting they are times 'when people may seek refuge in pre-established beliefs and in familiar models of activity' (1991). This is a similar claim to that made by Jackson and Warin (2000), who point to the role of gender as a long established aspect of self that may provide reassurance and self security during transitional times in a person's life such as the move from one phase of schooling to another. Simon's responses are aptly characterised in this way, presenting a clear illustration of this argument. His faith in sporting activities to help him to rehabilitate himself is a good example. He seemed to have fallen back on a long entrenched aspect of his story of self concerning his prowess at sport, especially running. He told me early on in this interview, with an obvious sense of pride, that he now visits the local gym almost daily (where he can get a 'child' rate until he turns eighteen). Here he did 'weights, running, swimming, all sorts' with the particular aim of 'building up my muscles'. He also told me he now attends self-defence classes and plays football in a local team twice a week.

It seems characteristic of Simon's literal-mindedness, his concrete thinking, that his improved sense of physical strength was giving him a stronger self image. Giddens (1991) suggests that fateful moments can be characterised as 'periods of re-skilling and empowerment', which again seems to fit with Simon's attempts to expand on his sporting abilities, selecting sports that would bolster him physically and defend his self. During the course of the final interview Simon volunteered the idea that the traumatic incident had turned him into a 'better person'. When asked to try to explain this further he said, 'A stronger person – like inside'.

Giddens suggests that fateful moments can also be characterised by the bringing in of experts. He goes further, suggesting that 'quite commonly, in fact, expertise is the vehicle whereby a particular circumstance is pronounced as fateful' (1991:114). This was certainly how Simon constructed this key episode in his life and how others, according to his account, have responded to it. Shortly after the attack, with support from school staff, he received therapeutic assistance from the Schools Psychology Service. This took the form of a weekly meeting in his home over several months, focused on helping him overcome his fear of going back into school. These meetings created precisely the kind of frequent and focused context for the telling of self that may have been lacking in Simon's life up until then. They gave him further opportunities for strengthening his self and building identity capital.

Evidence of a 'stronger' self

Martin, we saw, valued authenticity of self. Simon did not express anything resembling this value during his early adolescence. It was only in my conversation with him at age seventeen that I recognised the same implicit valuing of authenticity – a wish to be 'the self one truly is', as Rogers puts it (1995). I glimpsed this belief during our discussion of his comment about his peer group being 'a funny lot':

> JW: What kind of things do you [the group] do to make people laugh then?
>
> S: Well it's not me that makes people laugh. It's all them [his mates] . They do. They *change* [said with emphasis]. As soon as we're on our own we're alright but as soon as there's everyone out, they just click and change. It's weird. It's like you're alright, then, next minute with a click of fingers: change. Not the same person.

> JW: Because of the group?
>
> S: Yeah. Cos of the group. Like making people laugh.
>
> JW: So what happens to you then – with that click?
>
> S: I just go 'Right – I'll go somewhere else...I go 'right – I'll just go and get a football.
>
> JW: I think you are saying that when people are in a group – this 'click' thing – they change.
>
> S: Yeah. They change.
>
> JW: So do you not change then?
>
> S: No. I just stay the same – me. I just stay the same old person. It's just so weird how they do it though. It's like – go over to them and that's instant – change.

As Rose (1997) observes, the desire to be 'the same old self' is strongly embedded in everyday discourse about being true to, or discovering, ourselves. To acknowledge that one has changed seems to undermine the idea that you might be the same person underneath. In a study about the transition to university, based on interviews with 24 male undergraduates, Warin and Dempster (2007) found that several students expressed discomfort over the problems they experienced in 'putting on a front' or 'adopting a persona' at the start of their university career to become accepted in their peer group (p897). Simon's discussion of the 'weird' way his friends 'click and change' when they are together as a group 'when there's everyone out' compared to how they behave 'when we're on our own' draws out this underlying value for an authenticity of self. Simon distances himself from this behaviour emphasising a value for a consistency of self 'I just stay the same old person'. The value for a continuous consistent self implicit in this phrase seems to be interlinked with Simon's perception that he has emerged from the 'attack' incident as a 'better person' with 'more self confidence'.

Conclusion

Comparing Simon with some of the other children, especially Martin, I did not really see any evidence of a capacity to tell a story of self until the conversation we had, some time after the attack, when he was aged seventeen. During pre-school, Reception class and year 1, Simon seemed quite solemn and at times a little insecure, especially in larger peer groups. When asked about how he had changed, he responded in the concrete ways that typify this age group, emphasising activities and skills. When questioned more specifically about his self perceptions and changes in the interviews held in year 8, at age twelve to thirteen, he found it hard to respond to the abstract nature of the questions and showed little emotional literacy. It was only at age seventeen, reflecting on the impact of a 'fateful moment', the attack he had experienced, that he could articulate feelings about his self confidence and changes in his self perception. He seemed to have set out to strengthen his self, after the impact of the attack, through literally strengthening his body. However, he also had the opportunity through frequent therapeutic talks with a professional, and perhaps also with his parents and siblings, to reflect on his identity and to create it. Evidence that he had to some extent achieved this could be glimpsed in his valuing of self authenticity, for being the 'same old self'.

There was no doubt that the incident referred to as 'the attack' had a significant and deleterious impact on Simon's educational achievement. He left school at sixteen with one GCSE, in Art. However, viewed from the perspective of a focus on Simon's sense of self and developing self awareness, this pivotal event prompted a telling of self and adoption of strategies aimed at 'strengthening' his identity. In many respects this fateful moment acted as a springboard for developing the identity capital that Simon had been lacking.

9

Jayne's story: a roller coaster
of self confidence

Introduction

A notable feature of Jayne's story was the roller coaster nature of her self confidence, a term that recurred throughout the data I collected with, and about, her. Superficially, and to those who did not know her well, she appeared to be lacking in self confidence or self esteem, especially during the early years of school, a perception that may have been linked to her quietness and her small stature. She suffered from a slight speech impediment until she was about seven which made her shy about speaking directly to staff. On a closer acquaintance, however, Jayne seemed to be an emotionally secure person, especially during her years at secondary school, where her pro-school attitude gained favour with teaching staff and with a group of other girls, who shared this approach. Jayne's story also highlights her almost exclusively female world of home and school peer group and her exclusion of boys, whom she regarded as 'idiots'.

Self esteem is often discussed as if it were a fixed global characteristic. Jayne's story illustrates how significant changes in self esteem and its relative, self confidence, occur over time. For example I noted a gradual increase in confidence of the shy, quiet child I met at age four through to the newly appointed proud Head Girl I met in year eleven. Yet an ambivalence about her own abilities resurfaced when we were re-acquainted at age seventeen when she explained why she had chosen not to go into further education. As well as illustrating changes over time, her story shows how self esteem and self confidence (Jayne's own preferred term) are situation specific. She made comparisons with her peer group, especially her best friend Mandy, regarding her self confidence, as well as with her younger self. In our final conversation when she was aged seventeen, she was able to articulate an understanding that she was lacking in self confidence in some situations but not in others, so presenting a sophisticated and nuanced story of self.

Dressing up – the beginnings of self awareness

When I look back at the video recordings made in Brompton nursery (also attended by Simon, see Chapter 7), I note that four year old Jayne is frequently dressed up in clothes and hats from the nursery's rail of dressing up clothes. She wears a large black straw hat, with fake flowers in the brim, which falls down over her eyes, and a yellow silk dress that is much too big for her. These favourite items and others (a blue frilly dress, white felt hat, sundry necklaces, bags, and high heeled shoes) pop up again and again in the early recordings. Her obvious enjoyment of dressing up interested me, as I speculated that it might have some bearing on her developing sense of self. To what extent, I wondered, was she imagining how she might appear to others? Or were her choices based simply on a sensory enjoyment of texture and colour?

When I asked Jayne the question I asked all the children, about their preferred activities and toy choices in the nursery, she responded instantly and clearly 'Putting clothes on'. This reminded me of myself at the same age, when I spent much time enjoying dressing up, usually as an element of socio-dramatic play, using clothes and props to help me pretend to be other people. It was often the case that the children in the study evoked aspects of my own childhood and influenced my emotional response to them, bringing about feelings of identification or alienation, as discussed in Chapter 4. Jayne's love of dressing up enhanced my interest in and curiosity about her. Some of her dressing-up activities were incorporated into pretend play with her peers, often used to signal the taking up of a particular character, 'I'll be the doctor'. But Jayne seemed to be suggesting it was the activity of selecting and putting on clothes itself that was important to her.

Years later, when I discussed the video recordings with thirteen year old Jayne, she drew my attention to the consistency of her enjoyment of dressing up. I asked her 'Did you have any bits in it (the video) where you thought: 'that's really like me now?'' She responded: 'When I was dressing up, cause I like dressing up now', constructing it as a central characteristic that had stood the test of time. Her mother made a similar observation about this key attribute: 'She was always dressing up, always, and she still hasn't changed now. She likes all fancy clothes and girly clothes'. Also notable in my final conversation with Jayne at the age of seventeen was what she said when describing her self image:

> I'm for fashion and things. I've always got the latest fashion. I try my best to look nice. I won't go out of the house without makeup and hair straightened. I'd never wear trackies [track suit trousers]. I'm for high heels and handbags. Latest fashion.

The video recordings of Brompton nursery allow me to explore the young Jayne's enjoyment of dressing up and speculate on what it meant for the development of her self-awareness.

> Jayne is in the long yellow dress and a velvet hat. Another girl, Hayley, is standing close to her, also wearing a big hat. The two of them climb into the 'bus' [blocks arranged as seats on a bus with a steering wheel set up at the front]. Jayne assumes the driving seat. Mrs Harman's voice is heard saying 'Do you want to play outside anybody? Jayne quickly gets out of her dress and hat, puts them back on the clothes rail, then runs to get her coat. (Notes on video recording Brompton Nursery, June, visit 8)

> Jayne is sitting with Marie. They are close to each other and speaking in low voices. Jayne gets up and goes over to the clothes rail. She struggles into a frilly blue satin dress. She gets a hat as well before rejoining Marie. They both jump up and run off to the Quiet Room. They return with a doll. They are joined by two more children, a boy and girl, and there is animated talking which I cannot decipher. Jayne gets her necklace out from underneath the neckline of the dress. She plays with this, arranging it and looking pleased. (Notes on video recording, Brompton Nursery, July, visit 10)

These notes indicate that the clothes are operating as a kind of currency in establishing the social relationship between Jayne and her companions. It seems likely that Jayne and Hayley have recognised, intuitively rather than through any verbal negotiation, a common interest in the clothes rail. As I showed in Simon's story, and as many commentators on young children's play have observed, there is considerable overlap between young children's selection of playthings and of playmates. For example a fascinating account of young children's play drawn from an ethnographic study by Kantor *et al* (1998) shows how a small group of children establish an 'ingroup' through the shared development of their own play culture based on their symbolic use of the classroom's rhythm sticks as superhero weapons. This play culture is inaccessible to children who fail to understand and recognise the symbolic function of the sticks. Davies (1982) described young children's 'shared realities' as they construct their own cultures with each other. Dressing up established a shared peer culture for Jayne and her peers.

Jayne's choices of toys and activities compounded her exclusively female choices of playmates, reflecting the female dominated world of her home. At home the influence of her older sisters meant there was a ready supply of Barbie dolls as well as make-up and activities associated with the female pop world. She also had her doll, 'Baby Shivers', who accompanied her everywhere and was the focus of much nurturing play. At pre-school and later when she started at Brompton primary school, she frequently played with the domestic toys and dolls in the home corner, usually alongside other girls. She seemed completely oblivious to the boys in the class, as if they were filtered out of her field of awareness. Much later on, at the age of fifteen, Jayne was quite explicit about identifying the boys in her year group as 'outgroup', as 'idiots' with whom she did not want to work.

Why was the young Jayne so drawn to fashion, and dressing up? Was she just attracted to fabric, sparkly jewellery and hair bobbles because these things are intrinsically attractive and colourful? Or was her concern with her physical appearance indicative of her awareness of how she appeared to others – the beginnings of the 'me' self that develops when a person starts to become aware of and concerned about how others perceive them? Whilst 'self consciousness' is often described pejoratively, overlaid with a moral judgement about vanity, it might suggest an early awareness of how one is perceived by others. It is difficult, though, to find conclusive evidence that Jayne was actually capable of the mental shift required to imagine how others might see her. Given her close relationship with her sisters, it seems that an interest in fashion, clothing, hairstyles and jewellery was very much part of their shared world and a currency through which they related to each other. Indeed, this is exactly how Miss Blackwell, Jayne's teacher during her first two years at Brompton primary school, interpreted Jayne's interests:

> Nail varnish, on her toes as well as her fingers. Hair always in a pony tail... seems older than she is. Older than six. Although she's six and her appearance is six, her sort of actions are more teenager type of thing. Her clothes are more teenager type clothes. The image is more teenage ... her sisters, I think, have a big influence on that. I don't think it's necessarily her at all.

Miss Blackwell probably subscribed to the popular discourse that children should not grow up too quickly and that childhood innocence should be preserved for as long as possible (see discussions in Burman, 2008 and Guldberg, 2009). Perhaps she equated teenage behaviour with a sexualised style of appearance, as she sounded quite disapproving, especially in her noteworthy observation that Jayne's teenager behaviour is 'not her', so implying Jayne is pretending to be somebody she is not. Interestingly, Miss Blackwell's comment is an excellent illustration of an assumption about an underlying belief in the authentic self, a belief that people should be who they are. Was Jayne merely copying her sisters and powerful celebrity females such as the Spice Girls, who were popular at the time and whose music the three girls listened to? To what extent was she aware of how she looked to others in her world, for example to her sisters?

An aspect of Jayne's life during year 1, her second year at Brompton primary school, throws some light on this aspect of her development. It, too, concerns her interest in personal appearance and possible ability to imagine herself as others might see her. Jayne had developed a small lump, a cyst, on her face and had a minor operation to remove it during the school term. Both Miss Blackwell and her parents were aware that the cyst might upset Jayne, possibly inviting teasing and even bullying. Jayne's parents, Helen and Kevin, told me that Jayne had talked about her classmates' observations about it. 'Kids used to say 'What's that lump on yer face?' She'd tell us this'. Clearly Jayne was well aware of her peers' remarks and reported their very words to her parents. So she was certainly aware of others' perceptions of her. Miss Blackwell was concerned lest Jayne's scar would become an object of interest for other children in the class after her operation, and worried lest Jayne might be unable to cope because of her 'shyness'.

Helen and Kevin also described how, when it first appeared, Jayne found a rather remarkable way of coping with the cyst. She told them that when children questioned her about the lump 'she used to say back to them: 'It's me cyst and I talk to it. It's me sister''. It seemed that Jayne was given the correct medical term and, recognising its phonetic closeness to the word 'sister', a salient and valued part of her world, she had transformed her lump into another sister – somebody she talked to. The story was consistent with Jayne's treatment of her doll Baby Shivers, who, according to Kevin, also provided a private audience for her. This account contributed to my impression of Jayne as a child who managed to protect herself to some degree through her internal fantasy world. The story is a good illustration of how children sometimes come up with highly imaginative and humorous ways of managing what might otherwise be a distressing situation. Both her parents and Miss Blackwell had recognised that Jayne's cyst could have invited unkind remarks from her peers. But Jayne demonstrated both awareness of her peers' perceptions and a way of managing them.

Since Piaget asserted that children are 'egocentric' until the age of about seven, there have been various re-workings of his experiments, particularly by Margaret Donaldson, that mean that it is accepted that children can be capable of understanding the perspectives of others at a younger age. This is especially so when the perspective taking involves what Donaldson (1978) described as 'human sense'. At six years one month old, Jayne certainly had the cognitive competence to realise how her cyst appeared to others. (She was that age at the time the cyst story was reported to me). Rather more interesting is her emotional capacity to present the cyst in a favourable light that maintained her confidence and gave her some resilience to possibly unkind comments from her peers.

Self esteem: ups and downs

In her overview of Jayne's first two years at school, Miss Blackwell commented on Jayne's need for reassurance. I had arrived at a similar view, based on my observations. I noticed that she tended to copy other children's activities rather than initiate her own, and that she acquiesced readily to suggestions or commands from staff. My observations in Brompton nursery showed she was quick to follow the rules and rituals she learned there, such as going to her peg to get her coat, replacing her dressing up clothes on the clothes rail when told it was time to go out outside, and seating herself quickly at the table at the appointed signal for milk and fruit. I sensed this ready compliance gave her a feeling of knowing she was doing the right thing.

When she started in the new environment of Brompton primary school, Jayne did not know the rules and my video recordings show that she appeared to be unsure what to do. Where should she dry her hands after playing in the water? Which apron should she use for water play? Which for painting? Where should they be hung up? These things took time to learn, alongside other new behaviours such as lining up, carefully explained by Miss Blackwell. Jayne was extremely co-operative. As such rituals and behaviours, which Kamler (1999) calls the 'schooling of the body', and which are commented on by Brooker (2002) and Fabian (2002) in their research on transition into formal schooling, became second nature to her, I witnessed her visibly relaxing, and smiling more. She wanted to do the right thing. I observed that her need to conform became even more pronounced in secondary school and earned her much teacher approval. At the end of her second year in Brompton primary school, Miss Blackwell confirmed my observation of Jayne's need to know and follow implicit rules, linking her need for compliance with her under-confidence. She described Jayne as: 'very under-confident, not sure of what she's doing, needs constant reassurance ... she is worried about doing the wrong thing. She needs that kind of reassurance: 'Yes this is fine, good, carry on.'

During her early years of primary schooling Jayne was perceived by staff as 'under confident', 'shy', 'timid, and 'a nervous little girl'. Her personal confidence levels were reflected in the pronounced speech difficulty she had when I first met her in nursery, and during her first year of school. She couldn't pronounce certain letter blends, much to her parents' anxiety. By the end of her second year at school, her spoken language had greatly improved, a change that Kevin told me he believed to have been influenced by peer pressure. Jayne had told her parents that she had received critical comments from her school friends. They had told her, she said, that she spoke like a baby.

Rather like in the incident of the cyst, we see Jayne recognising and responding to the critical perceptions about her held by others, revealing
her advancing self awareness. I noticed that Jayne spoke less often than
her peers and this may have been because she knew she had difficulty
making others understand her and was self conscious about speaking
like a baby. Jayne's speech impediment might have caused her to be
quieter than her peers and give Miss Blackwell and other staff the impression that she was 'shy' and 'a very timid little girl'. They treated her
in accordance with these judgments, so setting up a spiral of cautious-
ness in their relationships with her. Yet within other social relationships
Jayne devised ways of coping and compensating for her speech im-
maturity. Within the context of her family she seldom had to vocalise
her needs, as her sisters, Vicky and Gina, were quick to anticipate what
she wanted and respond to her, which both Miss Blackwell and Jayne's
parents saw as perpetuating the problem. With her peers she coped by
non-verbal interaction, copying and playing alongside them. I was
struck that she managed perfectly easily, and assertively, to request me
to tie her painting apron for her one day without using any words at all,
simply placing herself directly in front of me until I recognised what was
required.

Self confidence and self esteem are close relations, as Hattie (1992) and
Byrne (1996) both observe in their discussions of the differences and
similarities between the two terms. In Jayne's story they differed according to the context in which they were used. Jayne herself, as we shall see,
spoke about her 'self confidence', whereas Miss Blackwell used the term
'self esteem', typifying the professional educational adoption of the
concept. 'Now Jayne, I would say, is low in self esteem', she remarked
during Jayne's second year of primary school.

Self esteem is a problematic concept and one I have learnt to approach
with caution, especially when it is used by a teacher about a school
pupil. My mistrust comes from several sources. For one thing, within
the psychological literature about self esteem there is an attempt to dis-
tinguish between a pure description of self (self concept) and an evaluation of self (self esteem) (see Rogers, 1982, and Hattie, 1992 for discussion) that is based on a distinction originally put forward by James in
1890. This is an artificial distinction since statements about self are
always value laden. For example the descriptions produced by the chil-

dren in this study, such as 'popularish', 'cheeky' 'helpful', 'hardworking', 'a rat bag', cannot be presented as aspects of self concept that are distinct from aspects of self esteem. Emotional responses and moral judgments are embedded within these terms every time they are produced. So I have avoided 'self esteem' and its counterpart 'self concept' when making statements about the children in this study. I prefer to use the terms 'identity' and 'stories of self'; since they are broad enough to incorporate both the emotional and evaluative components of self descriptions (see Baumeister, 1986).

The second problem with the concept of 'self esteem', and the reason for my mistrust of it, is that it is often used to signify a global and fixed aspect of the self. This usage is based on the work of Rosenberg (1979), who argued for the concept of generalised or global self esteem. This way of theorising self esteem is increasingly criticised, alongside growing recognition that self esteem is multi-dimensional; that an individual's ratings of the various different aspects of their self are context dependent (see Marsh and Hattie, 1996). This critique of the fixed and generalised nature of self esteem matches the approach taken in this study, which recognises that self experiences and articulations are always situation specific.

Despite this increasing recognition and critique of older theories about self esteem, a legacy seems to remain in the way self esteem is used in simplistic judgements that sum up, or dismiss, individuals. The danger when such beliefs are communicated to and accepted by a child or their parents, is that they contribute to an 'entity' view of the self (Dweck, 2000). Dweck argues that an 'entity' view of the self suggests the self is innate and unchangeable and her research shows that when people believe their abilities and attributes are unchangeable they do not make efforts to change themselves. So she advises teachers and carers to avoid presenting judgements to children which imply that attributes such as self esteem are unchangeable. Some commentators have drawn attention to the frequency with which the term 'self esteem' is used by educational practitioners (Kahne, 1996; Emler, 2001), a trend typified by Miss Blackwell. Perhaps its appeal lies in its appearing to be a technical psychological term, for example, when a teacher uses it with a parent about their child – but it means little more than that the teacher has a good rapport with, and likes the child.

Jayne's level of confidence fluctuated. It changed at different phases of the fourteen years of the study and according to the social context she was part of at that moment. As a young child she was particularly under confident with regard to her school work. Her parents reported that she cried over some work she had brought home, worrying about the response of staff. She also gave herself low scores for the cognitive competence items in the Pictorial Scale of Perceived Competence and Social Acceptance (Harter and Pike, 1983) that I used when the children were aged six, items such as 'good at numbers', 'can read alone', 'good at spelling' and 'knows a lot in school'.

When I spoke with Jayne at the age of twelve during secondary school, she was clearly able to discuss issues about her self confidence in an emotionally literate way. Indeed this was a salient and explicit element in her story of self. For example, she told me she had deliberately tried to overcome her lack of confidence in the public setting of the classroom. She said she had been unable to put up her hand in class, even when she felt she knew the answers to questions. In a follow-up interview some months after this conversation, she felt she had changed as result of making deliberate efforts: 'I'm more confident now and I put my hand up in most lessons now'. She certainly did not subscribe to an entity view of her lack of self confidence.

During her second year at Northend secondary school, Jayne's lack of confidence had clearly been recognised as requiring some action. Staff urged her to attend the school club that was specifically aimed at improving children's social skills and raising their self confidence. I formed a favourable impression of the school's promotion of social skills and the ways they supported Jayne and brought her out, glimpsed through her own positive account. She was glowing with pride when she revealed she had been given an award for her participation in the club as a 'social skills superstar'.

Jayne was able during this, her thirteenth year, to offer me a description of how her self confidence had changed over time and a nuanced description of her self confidence based on social comparisons with others. Her immediate reference group, that is the people with whom she was most likely to make social comparisons, included her 'best friend' Mandy and one other close girl friend, Bev. She volunteered several direct comparisons of their respective levels and types of self confidence. So, whilst she recognised that her confidence had grown, she was careful in positioning herself along an implicit self confidence continuum. It was not the kind of confidence that the 'more outgoing' Mandy possessed: 'Compared to Mandy and Bev, I was shy. Mandy will speak to anyone'.

In a discussion about her future aspirations, I asked if she would be prepared to leave the town and live elsewhere. She replied firmly and contrasted herself with Mandy. 'I'd stay here. I'd want to be around my family. Not like Mandy. She'd go anywhere'. It is interesting to take a closer look at Jayne's construction of the ways she differs from Mandy, as they provide insight into her underlying values. Whilst she might have admired and even envied Mandy's willingness to 'go anywhere' and 'speak to anyone', this was tinged with a slightly pejorative view of these qualities, as if it meant Mandy was undiscerning. Through this process of comparison with Mandy she produced nuanced statements about how her confidence had grown but that she was still not 'outgoing', a term she used twice. Ambivalence about her self confidence continued to be a theme in Jayne's life and, interestingly, re-emerged in the final interview with her at age seventeen.

From pro school to promoting school

Of all nine children, Jayne was the most positive about school, and this remained an unusually consistent response over three changes in institution – from Brompton nursery, to Brompton primary school to Northend secondary school. Her positive approach persisted from her first days at nursery and throughout her schooling, although her pro-school approach was focused more on school as a source of positive social relationships with peers and staff than on academic achievement. When I first met Kevin and Helen they told me that Jayne was thoroughly enjoying her nursery and was disappointed to find she couldn't go there on Saturdays. Her enjoyment of school came together with her love of dressing up in her enthusiasm for her school uniform, noted by Helen in her record of Jayne's first few weeks at school: she wanted to wear her uniform every day including at weekends.

Jayne's story of her school career provides a clear example of the entrenchment of a pro-school attitude (Lacey, 1970). For Jayne there seemed to be interdependence between two salient and positive aspects of her school career: her acceptance within a small well-established peer group that remained steady throughout, and the security she gained from teacher approval, which resulted in the ultimate accolade of being selected as Head Girl in year 11. Her secure place amongst her loyal group of girl friends, together with her positive relationship with her teachers, created a harmonious cycle of positive feelings about school. School, particularly secondary school, became a place where she felt a strong sense of belonging. Her small group of friends – Mandy, Bev and a few others – remained her social niche throughout her time at Northend school. As she remarked 'I just stuck to a few people'. Sociologists of school have shown how disharmony between peer acceptance and school acceptance creates an anti-school approach which can be exacerbated during the school career, whereas membership of a different kind of peer group can reinforce and bolster a pro-school approach (Lacey, 1970; Pollard, 2008). Jayne demonstrated a link between her positive relationships with teachers and her friendship with a small group of girls:

> J: We keep getting new teachers in, as teachers have been leaving but, yes, it's been good. I get along with them.
>
> JW: With all of them?
>
> J: Yes.
>
> JW: So do you think other people feel like that in school as well?
>
> J: Yes, well with my friends, my little group who I hang round with, yes.

Being part of a group of girls who shared the school-approved qualities of good behaviour, politeness and academic effort, meant that there was a strong accord between Jayne's peer group membership and her school membership. School was a place where she felt accepted, and recognised. Her preference to be in a small group of female friends, evident during my observations of her in the early years, continued throughout school. During a discussion about her choice of GCSE subjects, she was explicit about some of her choices being influenced by peer group issues: for one, her desire to have minimal contact with the boys in her year group, and for another, her identification with friends who shared a group identity as being 'mature'. It was in this discussion that Jayne othered the boys, stereotyping them as an outgroup: 'The boys are just annoying. They're idiots'.

The young Jayne, as we saw, gained a sense of security from having a conformist approach to school, and this carried on into secondary school where teacher approval and peer approval were mutually reinforcing. However, whilst Jayne's conformity gave her a sense of belonging and approval within the context of school, she hints that she may have paid a price for it. In her interview in year 8 of school she told me: 'At home I'm more myself than at school, you know. I want to do well and just be good and things'. She explains that at home you 'sort of let yourself go a bit. I feel more relaxed'. In saying 'more myself', she shows a value for an authentic self which is compromised by her conformist 'good' behaviour in school.

Jayne's conformist, good behaviour led to a significant change in school which she found very positive, especially with regard to the development of her self confidence. This change can be seen through the 'fateful moment' lens, that I also adopted to view a crucial phase of Simon's story (following Giddens, 1991). In Simon's case the fateful moment concerned a sudden and negative event that acted as a trigger for the construction of self. Whereas for Jayne her fateful moment confirmed her pro-school attitude and entrenched it further. The moment for Jayne was when she was chosen by the school to be their Head Girl. The decision was made at the end of the summer term of year 10, when she was aged fifteen and anticipating her final year in Northend (which had no sixth form). Meeting Jayne soon after she had been given this news, I could see she was very proud of this appointment, although 'shocked'. Her shock when her own perception of self collided with recognition of the staff's perception of her, indicates an experience of identity dissonance (see Chapter 4 for a description of this concept and Martin's story for an illustration of it).

> I wasn't going to put in for it and teacher said 'Oh yes, you've got to put in for it' and so I said, 'Ok I'll put in for Senior' [the role of Senior Pupil] and she came to me Monday and said, 'Oh I want you to be Head Girl'. Two of my friends, Bev and Katie, they wanted to be Head Girl, and they were really sure that one of them was going to be Head Girl, and it was me.

Jayne's reluctance to put herself forward for Head Girl was based on a subtle evaluation of herself in which she understood that she might meet the expectations of the Senior Pupil role, but she did not feel up to the status of Head Girl. She understood the hierarchical difference, explaining to me that the role of Senior Pupil was 'just the same thing really but the Head Girl, I don't know, it's just a bit higher'.

I was interested to find out how she would attribute her selection, and what her rationale for it would reveal about her story of self.

> JW: Why did she pick you?
>
> J: I was more mature than everyone else.
>
> JW: In what way?
>
> J: Getting me head down. I got me head down and worked.

By implication the social comparison she made in this conversation suggests she saw herself as the most mature pupil in the school. This was no doubt reinforced by Bev's and Katie's failure to be picked as Head Girl. The 'maturity' characteristic may well have been one the school staff provided as a justification for their selection but she certainly produced it as readily as if it had become an internalised self perception.

The Head Girl role took Jayne a step beyond her pro-school approach to a position where she was actively promoting Northend. Up until then she had been in favour of school life in general and her own school in particular. Now she had to externalise this value, as her new duties involved her in selling the school to prospective parents and pupils. Whilst she had developed a certain degree of self confidence through the school's social skills club, she now had to harness this quality to represent her school in various public settings. She clearly felt she had risen to the challenge.

> 'It was really good. Looking after younger children and representing the school. Showing new pupils round'.

She was made Head Girl during an interesting time for the school, as it had been placed in special measures by the Office for Standards in Education (Ofsted), a classification for schools where standards were deemed to be inadequate and therefore required a period of monitoring. Jayne reported:

> I took part in discussions about the school. We had to talk to inspectors about it. It was just coming out of special measures. We were trying to persuade people it was a good school. Which it is. Definitely.

142

Looking back on secondary school and comparing with primary school, Jayne was generous in her praise of Northend. She attributed the improvement in her self confidence to the school: 'It's given me more confidence to do things'. My observations and perceptions of Jayne indicated that, although Northend school took a pro-active role in helping Jayne to develop her social skills, it was her own willingness to acknowledge this agenda and make deliberate efforts to improve her confidence that accounted for the positive changes she recognised. Jayne did not subscribe to the idea that self confidence was a fixed quality.

Beyond school – threats to status, identity and belonging

With such positive feelings about school, how would Jayne approach the move away from an environment to which she felt such a strong sense of belonging? Studies of transition from one phase of schooling to another reveal the experience of transformation from 'top dog' to 'bottom of the pile', as identified by Simon in Chapter 7. Studies show that pupils are often anxious about the unknown that awaits them (Lucey and Reay, 2000). Warin and Muldoon (2009) found that pupils also feel that they are themselves 'unknown' to others in new and unfamiliar settings. Although this can occasionally be a positive feeling, a chance to reinvent oneself, it is more often experienced as a loss of identity and status coupled with anxieties about competence and recognition (Henderson *et al*, 2007). Jayne did not explicitly state that she would miss her status, as Head Girl, but it seemed very likely, given her pride and pleasure in this role and the strong sense of belonging she had articulated about her school years, especially in its final phase. It had been 'really good', she told me.

At fifteen Jayne anticipated that leaving school would be 'scary'. 'I don't know what I want to do', she said, trying to visualise what lay ahead. She may have been scared not so much of the unknown world awaiting her after school but of her own uncertainties about what she would like to do, who she would like to be, the unknown in herself. Perhaps she was afraid of being a nobody, after a high profile in school that made her a somebody.

Two years later at seventeen, Jayne echoed her statement of uncertainty about her future self. By then she had a job, but she was dissatisfied with it and still unclear about her future path and the idea of further education. The possibility of college compounded her uncertainties about identity, as 'nothing stands out that I want to do'. In Shelley's case we saw her goal driven approach to life after school, her strong sense of future, or future time perspective (FTP). Engler (2008) points out that the search for occupation during late adolescence is a vulnerable time for the construction of self, since it threatens the experience of being a productive member of society. It was this sense of a future and status in society after school that Jayne seemed to lack so totally when we had our final meeting.

Jayne was very dismissive about the job she had secured on leaving school. She was working as a room attendant in a hotel and perceived this as 'not a very good job'. She tried to play down the changes this had made to her life in a way that reminded me of how she had underplayed the transition from primary to secondary school. I asked what she had been doing since we last met. 'Starting work. Not major'. Later when she was more relaxed, she said more about her job, and her feelings about it: 'Boring. It's a maid basically. Making it nice for guests to come in'. She also told me, 'I got the job in August. Straight after school'. I wondered if she told me this because she felt some pride at getting a job so quickly, even though she did not rate it. She may also have emphasised the speed of her employment because she recognised that she might have acted too hastily. My lasting impression of this conversation was Jayne's statement: 'I regret not going to college'. Towards the end of our talk she came up with a new career idea that was satisfyingly consistent with her longstanding interests: 'I wouldn't mind working in a shop. Get into retail. Clothes'.

Speaking with Jayne for the final time, I was curious to know whether she had changed her views about boys. Did she still consider them to be 'idiots'? Had she developed any sexual or romantic relationships with boys? Looking back on her friendships at school she reinforced her earlier low opinion of her male peers: 'Stupid ones in our year'. She said she had had a boyfriend but 'Not any more. I found out he cheated on me'. So, it didn't look as if her opinion had changed very much.

During this final interview I noticed that Jayne again demonstrated a sophisticated way of positioning herself in relation to others when she constructed particular aspects of her identity. She observed that she was 'louder' in the company of her friends than when she was with her mother. She then went on to distance herself a little from the idea that she might be considered too loud by saying 'I'm not loud loud'. This careful positioning was similar to the way she had described her confidence in relation to her more outgoing friends. It also seemed in keeping with her positioning in relation to the roles of Senior Pupil and Head Girl. Jayne seemed to be wanting to tell a story of self in which she was aware of subtleties and nuances in relation to key attributes such as 'loudness' and 'confidence'. I felt it was important to her to position herself accurately as she told me her story of self.

Conclusion

As a young child Jayne's development of a 'me' self was created particularly through her interest in her personal appearance, probably spurred on by her older sisters and family culture, and through her awareness of how peers might perceive the cyst on her face and her baby-like way of talking. She was clearly concerned with the idea that others were aware of, and forming judgements about, her appearance. Confidence and self esteem were of interest to others in her early childhood world and became of central interest to Jayne herself when she began secondary school. Her story challenges research that treats self esteem as an unproblematic 'global' concept. She held a strong value for making an effort, 'getting her head down', which was part of her pro school approach. She also adopted this approach to the business of improving her self confidence, accepting the help Northend offered through their social skills club.

Fortunately for Jayne, she had not internalised the entity or fixed view of self esteem, nor the low self esteem portrayed by Miss Blackwell in her early school years, but recognised at secondary school that she could put effort into improving her self confidence. When I met Jayne at seventeen she was feeling insecure about her current job and about her future, contrasting this with the secure feeling of belonging she had enjoyed at Northend secondary school. But by this time she had developed a well differentiated understanding of herself, based on her recognition that she behaved differently with different people in different settings. Her capacity to tell a nuanced and differentiated story of self will be an asset to her as she faces her future.

10

Liam's story: social disadvantage and identity capital

Introduction

Liam's childhood was the most socially disadvantaged of all of the children in the study. This Chapter seeks to reveal the dimensions of disadvantage in his life and look at how they were interwoven with his story of self. A question within all the stories told so far concerns the way that social class influences the production of identity. Liam's story allows the concept of identity capital to be explored: the stock of insights that are drawn together to create a story of self. Sociologists suggest that the kind of introspection implicated in the production of identity is the privilege of those who have the time and space to engage with it. For example Coté (1996) claims that a higher social class background creates an advantage for the acquisition of identity capital whilst Skeggs (2004) suggests that the accumulation of the knowledge, experiences and opportunities necessary for the building of a self are not available to everybody. Henderson *et al* (2007) point out that 'individuals are not simply free to choose who and what they want to be' (p14). Liam's life was particularly constrained through multiple disadvantages and his story challenges the idea that all children have equal choice and scope for creating identity. To what extent did Liam have the opportunities, experiences and freedom he needed for telling his story of self?

147

Multiple social disadvantages

It is helpful to look at the six dimensions of child wellbeing set out in the UNICEF report on child poverty across 21 rich countries (UNICEF, 2007). These are: material wellbeing, health and safety, educational wellbeing, family and peer relationships, behaviours and risks and subjective wellbeing.

Let's begin with material wellbeing and economic comfort. A significant element of Liam's story was the poor quality and instability of his family's housing. When I first met him, aged three, he was living with his mother, Donna, and her parents in a small terraced house close to the brand new purpose built social services nursery he attended, the Osborne Centre. Seven years later he had moved into a council housing estate with Donna, young sister Kimberley and her father, Jason, then his Mum's long term partner and Liam's step-father. A few months later, following the separation of Donna and Jason, he had moved into a caravan park, and then on to another one whilst waiting for a council house. Finally Donna, Kimberley and Liam were housed in a council house on the Banks housing estate. For most of Liam's life his mother was not working. After mental health problems were diagnosed – she and Liam both informed me about her depression – she received disability benefit.

Next take health and safety. Liam and his sister might have been vulnerable because of their mother's mental health problems, but Donna's father, Liam's granddad, often stepped in to the breach, for example when Donna spent several weeks in hospital when Liam was sixteen.

With regard to educational wellbeing, Liam began missing a lot of school when he was thirteen and was moved to a Pupil Referral Unit. He never re-entered mainstream school, leaving the PRU at fifteen with no qualifications. Family relationships were also problematic. The separation of Donna and Jason left Liam feeling angry towards Jason and protective towards Donna and Kimberly. His peer relationships gave Liam an escape from the demands of school and home but compounded his anti school approach, especially during his mid teens. His behaviour at this time reflected classic teenager 'risky' behaviour, the fifth dimension listed by UNICEF: he informed me he was missing school, smoking cannabis and participating in local gang culture.

Liam appears to have led a life characterised by the classic indictors of social disadvantage, adding up to the 'multiple deprivation' identified in social policy, where the various strands of disadvantage are understood to have a compounding effect on each other (Social Exclusion Task Force, 2007; Toynbee and Walker, 2008). The value of the longitudinal case study approach presented here is that it can offer a critique of such rather simplistic unitary measures, and also examine how they relate to Liam's construction of self.

My strong impressions of the many compounding social disadvantages surrounding Liam were shaped through the long lens of my meetings and conversations with him during the entire course of the study. Whilst these disadvantages were an important part of the social context in which he grew up, they were not always salient in every meeting. He often came across as happy, he was willing and co-operative, and I felt we got on well. He also spoke, on occasions with pride, about his various skills and achievements. However, when I last met Liam at age seventeen he was wholly aware of the disadvantages he had accrued. Although he had spent a few weeks working as a labourer for a friend's dad in a roof insulation business, he was receiving the Jobseekers Allowance, the UK benefit available to unemployed people seeking work. So technically Liam was one of the growing number of young people with NEET status (not in education, employment or training). Layard and Dunn, (2009) estimated that 6.5 per cent of sixteen year olds in the UK had such status in 2006, and this figure has since increased with rising unemployment.

Liam made two strong statements on this occasion which coloured my abiding impression of this last visit. Firstly, he said he had 'hated school' and considered teachers to be his 'enemies'. He expressed deep anger about his school career. Some of the data from his younger days shows clearly that he had then held a different and altogether more positive view of school, especially during his first two years at Forest Hill High School. Longitudinal qualitative research can reveal this kind of re-telling when past events are influenced by the knowledge and feelings of the present moment (Thomson *et al*, 2003; Goodson and Sikes, 2001). Liam was re-writing history in the light of his present anger about his schooling.

Secondly, he made an unsurprisingly negative statement about his having no GCSE qualifications. He wished he had 'done some exams' because 'it's really hard to get a job with no exams'. These depressing, and depressed, perceptions from the seventeen year old Liam provoke questions about his life. How could his life have been different? Are there ways in which he himself or others around him could have improved his fortunes? And since the focus of this book is on identity, how was his developing sense of self implicated in shaping his life chances? Could he have done better if he had, for example, had more identity capital, the stock of insights that create a persistent story of self?

The onset of an anti-school attitude

Absence from school had a major impact on Liam's school career, building up to his early departure from the school system altogether and consequent lack of academic qualifications. At what point in his school career did he start 'bunking off'? Was this the result of a longer standing anti-school attitude? I tracked back over the data from the earlier phases of the study to see when he changed his approach to school and what influenced this change.

Liam had attended the Osborne Centre pre-school provision for five mornings a week in the year before he started formal schooling. The centre was right next door to Bridge View primary school and had an adjoining playground where, along with his pre-school peers, he had watched the primary school children at play. He moved into Bridge View with enthusiasm. 'He never stops talking about school', his grand-dad told me. 'He enjoys coming to school ... he comes very readily', said his Reception class teacher Mrs James.

Mrs James' comment was particularly interesting because it contrasted with her own frank opinion that she did not actually enjoy teaching Liam. Indeed I collected a fair amount of data that shows that Liam's teachers in the early phase of schooling were not impressed by him or his family. Expressions of personal dislike by teachers were surprisingly strong. Mrs James, for example said:

> I would say he's settled into school but he's been very difficult to have in the classroom, very difficult to enjoy having in the classroom. Hopefully he doesn't know that but there's something about him. He can't concentrate, he can't listen... he didn't like that he had to sit for two minutes at a time or even

sit quietly. He couldn't cope with that at all, and you know, talking when other people are talking. He doesn't listen and he doesn't respond. It's like to talking to a brick wall.

Whilst Mrs James cites the difficulties that all children experience when they learn how to become school pupils, absorbing the expectations and the implicit and explicit classroom regulations, she seems to have experienced particularly strong frustration with Liam. The following notes, based on the video recording of Liam's first few days in the Reception class at Bridge View, show he was behaving in ways that were unlikely to endear him to staff. He could not perform well on the base line measures of school readiness that were being used at the time, such as knowledge of colours and counting. He could not apply himself for long to a task set by the teacher and made matters worse by saying 'I can't do it'. He preferred boisterous noisy forms of play with his peers, which brought reprimands from staff:

Mrs James asks Liam to draw a picture of himself. He says 'I can't'. Then he tries. Then he hands the paper to Mrs James to show he's done enough. Mrs James clearly isn't satisfied. She asks him to talk about it. 'That's me that' he says. Later he is threading beads with some absorption. Mrs James comes and sits very close beside him. She asks him about colours and he fails to identify them correctly. (Notes from video recording, Bridge View primary school, Sept, Visit 1)

Mrs James asks him to draw a picture of himself (as she did yesterday – her second attempt). Liam sits sucking his pencil and not getting on. Mrs James leaves him to do the picture by himself. Liam looks uncomfortable but does some vigorous crayoning. Then he stops. Mrs James returns. He re-applies himself but gets very distracted. Then he says 'I can't do it'. He sits sucking his pencil and then rolling it down his head and pressing his head. (Notes from video recording, Bridge View primary school, Sept, Visit 2)

Liam is with Callum and David in the playhouse/home corner. Callum is shooting with his arm. He addresses a fourth boy who has joined them. 'We are Power Rangers' [said in a super-hero American accent] 'and you are not'. Then Callum rushes out saying 'It's morning time'. Liam follows. They move off making kick movements [Power Ranger style]. Mrs James calls them over to her. 'Now then you boys, are you just wandering around making a noise?' She tells them to take some toys back to the playhouse where they are supposed to be kept. They rush off at once and she has to call them back very sternly and reprimand them for running. (Notes from video recording, Bridge View primary school, Sept, Visit 3)

My earlier observations of Liam in the Osborne Centre noted his engagement in aggressive play. My notes from the nursery in the summer before he commenced formal schooling included for example, scratching another child, pushing another child in the face, and a lot of pretend sword fighting with the construction toys. However, this behaviour had either been tolerated or gone unnoticed by the staff there. Staff at Bridge View had different expectations. Mrs Mason, who followed on from Mrs James and taught him in his second year of school, held equally negative views of him. She, too, was frustrated by his inability to learn the school's expectations about behaviour: 'He's not aware he's being naughty'. She also said, disturbingly, 'He's the sort of child you don't get to know', attributing her lack of knowledge to a deficit in Liam rather than in herself.

These negative impressions of Liam reported by staff during his early years of school were compounded by their disapproval of Liam's mother and their doubt about her competence as a parent. Mrs James drew attention to Donna's youthfulness and described her as 'weak':

> I've had to have chats with Mum because he's been naughty, very naughty [elaborated as his inability to sit still and his constant talking] ... I got the impression from Mum that it was 'Oh, I don't really know what to do about it' you know, very weak. She's young, but other people are young but it was more, weak really, and I got the impression Liam was given the rule of the house, no boundaries set at home.

Mrs Mason saw her as a young mum and associated this with her inability to provide discipline.

> I get the feeling that he's perhaps a bit spoilt at home and that – I don't really know. I mean I see his mum a lot in town on her own with him. She seems very young, and I just wonder sometimes whether he's not really getting very much discipline.

Such comments by the teachers, together with my observations of Liam's relationships with staff, show that he was identified as a rather difficult child, from a difficult background, who was unlikeable. How far was Liam himself aware of these negative views? It is quite possible, as we saw in Shelley's story, that teachers disguise their negative attitudes to the children they teach. Teacher professionalism militates against strong personal likes and dislikes (which is why the comments about the young Liam seem unusually frank). This, plus the behaviour re-inforcement techniques primary school staff often choose to operate mean that the staff who professed to find Liam unlikeable will have tried to disguise their feelings by taking a 'positive' approach to him (see Wheldall, 1991 and the recommendations of the Elton report, DES, 1989). As Mrs James says during the Reception class year:

I've had to be really nice with him even though there wasn't much likeable about him. He's been behaving because of it. He didn't want to please before. Now he's beginning to show signs of wanting to please.

So it seems likely that Liam, like Shelley (Chapter 6) was fortunately un-aware of the negative views the staff held of him and his family. His response to school, then, was positive in these early years.

There is another way in which Liam's life might have been different, especially with regard to his attitude to school. He had a hearing problem but this was not diagnosed until the end of his second year at school. Donna explained what had happened when I spoke with her at the beginning of Liam's third year. Liam had just had grommets put in his ears and this had had a 'brilliant' outcome. But when Liam was experiencing hearing problems in the first and second years of primary school, nobody acted to help him. The hearing issue certainly impacted strongly on the unfavourable responses towards him from the primary school staff. Both Mrs James and Mrs Mason commented about how hard he was to communicate with, an aspect of his personality that they seemed to link with their idea that he was 'not likeable'. Would it have made a difference to Liam's schooling if his hearing problems had been spotted earlier? Perhaps it could have led to considerable improvements in his interactions with teachers and a more friendly and positive response from them. However as we have seen, the teachers' impressions of his lack of responsiveness might not necessarily have influenced their behaviour towards him.

So I have to look for the start of an anti-school approach at a much later stage. How far was this apparent during the interviews I conducted with him in secondary school when he was in year 8 (his second year) at Forest Hill High school? Had he started a habit of 'skiving' at that stage? Further evidence of a positive attitude to school, and a reasonably positive appraisal of school achievement was still present in the data I collected at that time. For example in his first interview from this phase he says 'Some lessons I'm not that good but most of them I am'. In Maths 'I'm in set 1 and that's the best set'. Liam showed me his school report, for the preceding year, his first at secondary school. This read, 'A very good report for Liam who seems to have settled down well this year'. All was well then with his school attendance during the initial phase of secondary school.

Piecing the story together from Liam's conversations during year 10 (age fifteen) and later, when he was seventeen, it seems that a pattern of school absence began to take hold some time after the split between Donna and her long term partner Jason, Kimberley's dad, and the family's subsequent removal to live in temporary accommodation in a caravan park. This was situated in a small town several miles from their previous house and, significantly for Liam, several miles from Forest Hill High School. Liam gave an account of these moves which links his school absenteeism to his worries about his Mum. He articulated the idea that his patchy attendance caused school to feel 'different' to him, and he was aware of others noticing his ongoing absences.

> I didn't want to leave my Mum in the caravan and that. I started staying in the caravan and then, when I used to go back to school, I don't know, it was just different. They didn't see me there for two days in a row. I'd be there for a day and then they wouldn't see me for week and then when I'd come back again people would be like, 'Oh, how come you're not at school?'

Liam went on to explain that the school provided various forms of support and transport to improve his attendance at this time:

> Sue Pearson, she's our err attendance lady, attendance, she used to take me to school when I was in Castle caravan park cos there wasn't a taxi there and Sid, a man, he's the welfare officer, Sid Roberts, he used to take me to school and Sue used to bring me back.

It seems that Liam was not developing an anti-school attitude at this time but was concerned with looking after his mother in their new and difficult circumstances. This had an unfortunate effect on his school attendance, which the school then tried to address through a range of support strategies.

By the time I spoke with Liam two years later, however, his attitude to school had changed dramatically. Liam, now aged fifteen, was living on the Banks estate. He believed that the consequent change in his peer group had a major influence on his attitude to school, as he then met others who were not attending school, so this became the norm. They would go into town together or visit a mate's house, something Donna seldom knew about. Staff at Forest Hill tried to get Donna to send him to school but, Liam told me, he 'just wouldn't go'. He also reported, significantly, that when he did go he was 'disruptive'. He was then asked to go 'the Centre' (his term for Cragside PRU). My attempts to construct a chronology of events with him suggest this was at the end of year 9.

Liam was at the PRU for three terms. He described his experience there focusing on his belief that the teachers there also saw him as troublesome. Unlike his unawareness of teacher perceptions of him in the early years of primary school, he was now well aware that he was seen as a disruptive influence. He explained that the PRU 'tried to reintegrate me' (into mainstream schooling) but 'I wouldn't go'. In the notes I made after this conversation I recorded 'he said this as if there was no choice'. At this point in the conversation he told me of 'a kid living near here who has not been to school since he was nine'. I felt this comment was offered to show me that his behaviour was not unusual on the Banks estate. His account portrayed a culture of school non-attendance within his immediate community.

Donna's account of Liam's school trajectory, following his removal to Cragside PRU, gives the brief facts:

> When he left Cragside he had a home tutor for four hours a week. For English and Maths. He didn't sit his GCSEs. He never returned to Forest Hill High school.

So, to speculate about the degree of inevitability of Liam's lack of school success it seems that a particularly critical phase was the time after the parental separation and consequent re-housing, establishing a pattern of school non attendance that laid the ground for identification with fellow school truants when he moved to the Banks estate, leading to school refusal and an eventual lack of exam qualifications.

Could things have been different for Liam?

We noted a number of family factors which could potentially be added to the list of social disadvantages in Liam's life. The list could include

Donna's sole parent status during Liam's early childhood and again during the middle years of adolescence (and consequent decrease in family income), the traumatic separation between Donna and Jason, and Donna's mental health problems. However, such a list of family disadvantages provides only a superficial view. The detailed approach taken in the case study method shows a more complex picture of Liam's family relationships, including some positive features.

A consistent theme running through Liam's contributions to our conversations concern his closeness to his family: an affection and admiration for his young sister Kimberley, a companionable relationship with his granddad Bill (Donna's father), and a protective and caring attitude to his mother Donna. Although Liam's relationship with his mother sometimes positioned him as a carer with responsibilities beyond his years – a concern of social policy (Aldridge and Becker, 2003) – this role may have been affirming for him. In addition my impression of seeing the two of them together on many of our meetings was of a mutual warmth and closeness. As we saw in Chapter 2, researchers interested in the components of resilience have speculated that positive family relationships can provide a form of protection for young people. Iacovou (2004) for example points to good family relationships as the key to the reversal of early disadvantages. Liam's family relationships warrant consideration to see how they compensate for and interact with the other social factors discussed, and how they contribute to his growing sense of self and his social awareness.

Liam was very open about his affection for Kimberley. She was three years old when I met Liam again after the seven year gap in our acquaintance. When constructing the time-line of events that had occurred since my last visit, he rated her birth as a significant event. He was demonstrably affectionate with her, took pleasure in telling me about the similarities between them, and seemed impressed, rather than threatened, by her 'smartness'. He told me she was 'good with numbers' and his equal when she played on his computer game. When Liam was asked to name three significant people in his life for the exercise I had devised to draw out social comparisons, he said: 'There's four, cause I've got my sister, my Mum and Dad (Jason) and Granddad. First would be Kimberley, cause I love her a lot. She's me sister'. When I asked him to select preferred family photos of himself, he chose several that portrayed the two of them together and which prompted good memories of shared games.

Liam's comments about the impact of Donna's separation from Jason offered further insight into the relationship between himself and Kimberley:

> I don't want to see him because I always stress out with him because he said, it must have been seven/eight months ago, he said to my sister on the phone 'I'll be here this weekend'. But he didn't come and that's why I don't like him. It's not upsetting for me because he wasn't my proper dad, but as it's my sister, my sister keeps saying, she was saying the other night, she was laid in bed for about two hours and not going to sleep and I said 'Go to sleep' and my sister goes 'I don't want to go to sleep. I want to talk about Daddy'... And you can't talk about him. I've seen him a few times but he's never stopped and talked. He's seen me but he never talks.

Liam became very protective towards Kimberley and although he denied that he was upset on his own behalf, his sense of betrayal surfaced in his remark that this 'Dad' now ignored him when they saw each other.

His granddad Bill was a key figure in Liam's life. When I spoke with Donna the last time I visited the family, Bill had recently died from a heart attack. She explained to me how deeply this had upset Liam, as they had had such a close relationship. I had realised this when Liam was younger and he had pointed out Bill whilst we watched the video recordings I had made of his pre-school: 'That's Bill. That's my granddad's name, that's who I used to play with all the time, like football'. My notes from the early phase of the study show that granddad Bill was a significant presence in Liam's life, often collecting him from pre-school and school, and Mrs James confirmed this impression: 'He never stops talking about Bill'. During the interview with Liam at age fifteen, he explained the value of his relationship with his granddad compared with his relationship with Donna, again revealing his protective feelings towards her. In answer to a question about who 'knows him best', he said:

> It's probably my granddad because if I open up about things to my Mum I think 'Oh I'm making it worse' but if I open up to my granddad I like, I don't know, it won't seem like he'll worry about it.

Liam mentioned that he had the chance to do woodwork whilst he was at Cragside PRU. He had enjoyed this and explained why:

> I liked it because my granddad did woodwork at school. And he was one of the best and I'm one of the best now. I was one of the best anyway, in my woodwork I could get every angle and everything right.

However he also identified with his granddad in way that helped to explain his indifference to the importance of school success:

> I used to skive school and when I used to skive school I didn't come home here [home]. I used to go to my granddad's, and my granddad would have a laugh and say 'skiving again', but he couldn't do anything because I didn't like school.

Donna, as we have seen, was described by primary school staff as a weak parent, yet all my contact with her family suggested that she gave Liam warm and continuing care, and his affection for her was clear throughout the conversations I had with him. But her own vulnerabilities meant he often perceived himself to be caring for her rather than the other way round. He showed strong loyalty to his mother in his account of why Jason remarried. His interpretation of events minimised the status of the new wife, in an attempt to protect Donna:

> My Mum was split up for six months and I think he [Jason] got a wife straight away. They got married and everything but that was because he didn't want to marry her, he just did it because he wanted comfort I think. He wants a woman around the house.

In the interview held in year 10, when Liam had been at Cragside PRU, he discussed his plans for his future schooling. He believed he was being required to return to his mainstream school. He knew about the legalities regarding his school truancy and acknowledged that this Mum could get 'done', though he believed that some of the problems the family had experienced would make this unlikely.

In recent years it has become commonplace to see media headlines bemoaning the lack of male role models and using this argument to explain various 'crises' of masculinity. The popular line of argument is that boys' academic success and employability would increase, and their criminal activity and poor behaviour decrease, if only they had more men about them in the form of involved fathers, carers and teachers.

Biddulph (2003) exemplifies this line of argument. A number of researchers have challenged this view (for example Skelton, 2001; Haywood and Mac an Ghaill, 2003), and concluded that it is not the gender of the adult carer that is important but the quality of care (Golombok, 2000). It is interesting to explore Liam's access to male adults and the role of father figures in his life in the light of this discussion.

Both Donna and Liam himself intimated that concerns about discipline were an issue within the family. Whilst providing a mainly positive view of Liam's relationship with granddad Bill, Donna maintained that he was 'too soft' on Liam. Liam himself hinted at considerable family conflict over his own behaviour, saying he believed it might have been a cause of the break-up between Jason and Donna, and revealing a conflict over their respective perceptions of him:

> He [Jason] couldn't cope with me. He couldn't cope with me then. But now I'm twice/three times as worse as I was but I'm not as bad with my Mum... I used to be a pain in the backside and then he couldn't cope with me ... That's what he thought. My Mum thought I was nothing, I was perfect. But to him I was like, I was always mythering him.

Liam reinforced the construction of himself as a challenge to paternal coping skills when he pointed out, wryly, that Jason's new marriage had brought about a worse situation with regard to controlling teenage children:

> He couldn't cope with me then but now he's got a fourteen year old and a sixteen year old to look after. That's what he brung on. He couldn't cope with me so I don't think he's going to cope with them. No way is he going to cope.

It is interesting to consider why Liam tells such a strong story about his stepfather's failure to cope with him and the implicit levels of conflict this must have entailed. Did he perhaps feel he was partly to blame for the family break up? It seems highly likely that he did, given his assertion about Jason's inability to cope and his awareness of the divergence in Donna's and Jason's views of his behaviour. His story is consistent with research that shows how frequently children blame themselves for parental separation (Oesterreich, 1996). Seeing beyond Liam's self blame, however, we get the impression of a stepfather who rejected him, no longer talking with him when they met, no longer interested in sustaining and developing rapport with Liam (if he ever was).

159

Clearly, Jason was not the 'good male role model' that popular discourse suggests boys require. Liam's story allows us to challenge the rather simple panacea of 'more male role models' that is currently prescribed by many policy makers as a cure for male under-achievement and anti-social behaviour. His relationship with his step-father provided a model of ineffective fathering and inability to cope, and his identification with his granddad Bill, whilst a source of comfort and affection, provided him with a model of indifference to school success and school attendance. The simplistic prescription for 'more male role models' does not take sufficient account of the *quality* of relationship between young males and their adult male caregivers and the types of masculinity that they offer.

Social reference groups: the role of peers

The influence of peers is significant when we consider how Liam's school trajectory might have produced more positive outcomes. Liam explained his poor school attendance and eventual non-attendance as partly due to his identification with others in his neighbourhood, on the Banks estate, who had a history of skiving school, an attitude compounded by granddad Bill's support. An affiliation with others in his neighbourhood became an important aspect of Liam's life, especially after he moved to the Banks estate. Sociologists of peer relations in adolescence describe the formation of group sub cultures through a process of 'othering', in which members of a group identify with each other and gain group cohesion and a sense of belonging through describing non members as 'other' (Hey, 1997; Epstein, 1993). In social psychology, the same process is described in terms of forming 'in-groups' and 'outgroups'. Tajfel, for example, emphasises the importance of group membership in forming identity. He suggests that we need to increase the status of any group we belong to, simultaneously decreasing the status of the 'outgroup', dividing the world into 'them' and 'us' (Tajfel and Turner, 1979). This approach has been applied to understanding the formation of adolescent peer sub-cultures (Cotterell, 1996; Swain, 2000; Sheriff, 2007). These ideas seem relevant to Liam's discussion of the two rival gangs, which began to dominate his life after he moved to a house on the Banks estate.

In answer to a question about his move to the estate, Liam articulated a sense of belonging to a group of Banks peers who hung around together in a nearby play area and went to play football outdoors. He contrasted this type of ingroup behaviour with the behaviour of an older acquaintance, positioning this older friend as an outsider.

> I like it round here. I know everybody. I do know everybody now, nearly everybody. I'm friends with anybody, like all the Banks, literally everybody ... I hung round with somebody from school first, who I know from school, and then, I didn't hang round with him anymore, because, I don't know, he doesn't do owt, just stays in and watches TV. He's not the kind of person who wants to go out and do things ... there's a big Astroturf and we normally go footballing there...

The Banks estate borders another housing estate known as Lindale. They are well known in the town for their rivalry and often associated with various kinds of trouble, including street fights, when hostilities surface in the relations between the young people who live in them. Both have a predominantly white working class population and do not appear to be very different in character, to an outsider such as myself. However, the residential membership of one or the other group bestows a strong feeling of belonging and sense of identity, which relies on these processes of group formation. Liam described events which illustrate a typical eruption of hostilities:

> The Banks and Lindale don't get on, you've probably read it in paper. The Lindale came round through here, it must have been about three or four weeks ago now, and they put houses windows through down that side. They knocked fences out of their gardens and ripped them out ... They came round in their vans and just did it ... It was alright, there was no fighting for about six years and then Ryan Jones's girlfriend, Kerry, her name is, she's related to both sides, she's related to the Banks and Banks people and Lindale people ... She had her eighteenth birthday on the rugby club, just up, as you go onto Banks, and it all kicked off...

These group dynamics are carried into the local schools that serve these two estates, creating another significant reason for Liam's unwillingness to attend school. He attributed his discomfort and 'stress' at school to these conflicts and to his minority status within Forest Hill school as a Banks resident.

> There's more Lindale in Forest Hill [Liam's first secondary school before his
> move to Cragside] than there is Banks. There's only, I'd say about my age
> group, altogether in Forest Hill there's about ten Banks people and Lindale,
> there must be about one hundred. I stress out on that; I had loads of fights
> at school because of it.

When I asked Liam what might have made his school life better, he replied: 'I don't know, just no rowing, completely no rowing but you
couldn't do that because there's more Lindale than Banks people'.

The membership of socio-cultural groups, and specifically of youth
sub-cultures, has an influence on personal constructions of self. Group
characteristics come to represent the individual and the individual can
be seen to represent the group (Tajfel and Turner, 1979). We have seen
this in the cases of the other children, for example Jayne's membership
of a pro-school group of conformist girls. However, Liam never characterised the distinction between the Banks group and the Lindale group
with any specific attributes. The distinction seemed to him to be entirely on territorial grounds. He had a sense of belonging, an experience
of 'us' (Banks) and 'them' (Lindale) but no particular group identity.
Whilst membership of the Banks estate gave him a sense of belonging,
the security of having a social niche, he did not articulate any specific
self descriptions through this group membership. Belonging to the
Banks group did not seem give him any identity capital, a concept I turn
to now.

Was Liam deprived of opportunities for creating a story of self?

Having untangled the various strands of deprivation in Liam's life, we
can consider whether he also suffered from a lack of identity capital, the
stock of insights that create a personal story of self. As we have seen, a
number of sociologists and psychologists have identified a subtle but
extremely important form of deprivation concerning the lack of opportunities for reflecting on and building up a self (Skeggs, 2004: Giddens,
1991; Coté, 1996; Rose, 1997). These authors argue that the construction
of identity is a privileged process engaged in by the middle classes. Is
this form of deprivation part of the multiple deprivations experienced
by Liam? Is it harder for somebody with the many social disadvantages
that characterised Liam's life to build up identity capital?

One factor relates to opportunities for the kinds of talk that help a person tell a story of self. This line of argument can be illustrated by comparing Liam's life with Martin's, for example, who had many more opportunities for the kind of abstract talk that produces a stock of rehearsed insights into self. Liam's poor school attendance, plus the fact that he spent much of his time in the company of peers rather than adults, may have limited his access to the discourse needed for building identity capital. The work of theorists who have researched the link between social class and language development, for example Barnes (1976), based on Bernstein's (1971) identification of an 'elaborated' language code, support this argument. However this discounts the range and diversity of Liam's social relationships. He spent time with his granddad, his young sister, his mother and also with his wider family, including cousins, and with his mother's friends. It would also be a rather simplistic dismissal of his peers to suggest they were incapable of conversing about social relationships, making social comparisons, and constructing insights about self and others. I have shown that opportunities for explicit verbalised self reflection can be created precisely because of disadvantageous circumstances through conversations with professional sources of support (Simon's story, Chapter 7).

My knowledge of Liam's life is based entirely on the accounts he chose to give me and there are many gaps. I realise I know little about his transfer to Cragside PRU, and the conversations with various professionals that would have been part of this process and that may have constituted opportunities for the telling of self. These events and the traumatic family break up referred to above will have created 'fateful moments', prompting self reflection and creating identity capital. However, in the interviews I conducted with Liam at ages twelve to thirteen, before these incidents took place, he was still reliant on concrete forms of self presentation and less able to tell an abstract story of self.

The most challenging strategy I used with the children when they were aged twelve/thirteen was to ask them to brainstorm a list of self descriptors, to 'bombard me with words that describe you' (see Chapter 5). Some found this quite easy and quickly produced a list of words that they could then explain. Martin, for example, showed an ability I characterised in his story as 'emotional literacy'. Others, such as Simon, found it altogether more challenging. Liam was extremely hesitant:

'Don't know really ... don't know really it's hard to think ... I don't know I can't think'. He resorted to the more concrete strategies used by younger children, describing his likes and dislikes and his abilities, and emphasising his sporting abilities: running, doing stunts on his BMX bike and roller blades. At thirteen, Liam also struggled to respond to the request to put himself in the shoes of significant others in his world and imagine how he might appear to them. For example when asked to imagine how Kimberley might see him, he started to describe how she liked jumping on top of him on the sofa, providing further evidence of an emphasis on the visible and concrete rather than the abstract, and suggesting he could not readily communicate her perspective. So Liam's responses to the strategies that were intended to prompt self descriptions seem to have met with a failure to articulate a story of self. This evidence would suggest that at this age he lacked identity capital, that he perhaps had an 'impoverished self' – the term used by Harter (1999) to describe children who lack the vocabulary or evaluative concepts to describe the self.

However although these rather direct strategies designed to elicit self statements were unsuccessful with the thirteen year old Liam, two years later, at fifteen, my experience of talking with him was rather different. Whist he was still inclined to dwell on the concrete aspects of events in his life, providing detailed descriptions of some of his activities, he was also able to communicate some highly self aware insights. For example he offered the view that he changed 'a lot' since moving to his new home. Although he then explained the changes in concrete terms again, talking about the change in activities from football to hunting, fishing and motorbikes, he gave animated, lengthy and highly technical accounts of these activities. He gave a vivid account of fishing trips with the boyfriend of his Mum's best mate, 'lamping' in the fields at night (hunting for rabbits) and hunting with ferrets. These were some of the lengthiest speeches made by any of the children throughout the years of the study and communicated his enthusiasm for the interests that were integral to his story of self.

Liam also produced several statements that showed he was clearly capable of imagining how he came across to others, and making social comparisons to create more abstract statements in constructing his identity. It was then that he used the term 'disruptive' to describe how he felt teachers at Cragside PRU saw him. At this stage, too, he could reflect back on the split between his mother and Jason and recognise that these important others in his life saw him in very different ways. His reflections on this traumatic separation also revealed self aware insight, when he reflected that he had selected an interpretation of events that protected his own feelings. In the account below he demonstrates his awareness of alternative narratives and his understanding that one of them helped him to avoid too much anger:

> I think it's because when we first moved in here he [Jason] came and he said that, to my Mum he said that he still loves her and that's what and every time he comes here when he goes he cries because he wants to be with us again and he knows his chances have gone. So that's why I think he doesn't come. Even if it isn't that, I'm trying to get into my head that it is because otherwise if he's just not coming because he can't be bothered then it would wind me up.

Liam recognised that he might have been deluding himself about his stepfather's motives for avoiding the family but preferred his optimistic interpretation so he could avoid the unthinkable idea that Jason couldn't 'be bothered' with them. So at thirteen he showed an empathic understanding of Jason, and also insight into and management of his own emotions.

During this same conversation he constructed a view of himself as easy to get on with: 'I just get on with everybody'. He then explained the statement in an interesting and quite sophisticated way, relying on social comparison with 'some people', and implicitly referring to discourses about social prejudice:

> I don't, like some people, see somebody in the street and just say 'I don't like him' straight away cos of like the way he's dressed.

Liam implies that others in his reference group are inclined to make quick judgements on the basis of dress or personal appearance whereas he is not. His story of self, created with me, includes this noteworthy claim to be free from prejudice.

Conclusions

As a child whose life was particularly constrained through multiple disadvantages Liam's story is a challenge to the idea that all children and young people are equally free to choose who and what they want to be. It offers a critique of the assumptions underlying Giddens' 'reflexive project of the self' that all have equal opportunity for creating identity capital. Liam was slower than the other children to develop the communicative capacity for presenting insights about self and others. By the age of fifteen, however, perhaps as a consequence of some of the more difficult incidents in his life, he had developed greater emotional literacy.

I don't know what will become of Liam. Of all the young people whose stories are told here, I am inclined to be most concerned about adverse outcomes in his ongoing life trajectory. His immediate neighbourhood has a reputation for high levels of crime amongst its young male population. However, this study has taught me that my predictions are often wrong, and that there are many surprise outcomes on the lifespan roller coaster. I am also aware that there are some protective factors in Liam's circumstances that might well work in his favour. His loyalty to his mother and sister, and his protective feelings towards them, whilst they may have created quite a burden of insecurity for a young boy, may help to motivate him as a young man and keep him out of trouble. They may, potentially, be a buffer or compensatory factor, and counterbalance the adverse consequences that ensue from a lack of educational qualifications.

I also have considerable faith in Liam's generosity of spirit, shown in the approach he took to working with me. My abiding impression of the young Liam was that he was forthcoming when I spoke to him, and responded cheerfully and co-operatively to my more formal interviews with him during his year in the Osborne Centre nursery and in the Reception class at Bridge View. During the middle phase of the study (the year 8 interviews) when he was aged twelve/thirteen, I was struck by his willingness to help. He was positive about my continuing interest in him, asking at the end of his first interview: 'will you come to see me again?' and commenting positively on the experience in later interviews.

Liam made an exceptional contribution to my key focus on the development of identity. His story has revealed instances of a clear and honest kind of self awareness. His words about the nature of change remain one of the most authentic responses to my difficult question about how he had changed during the course of secondary school: 'I can't see change because it's changed bit by bit and I can't see it'.

Section 3
Endings

My intention was to gain insight into the lives of the five young people through their stories and also into the nature of personal identity. In the next two Chapters I draw the two types of insight together and go on to ask the all-important question, 'so what'? I answer by suggesting how these insights might influence educational policy and practices concerned with improving children's wellbeing.

11
Hindsight and foresight

Although we can gain a good sense of the resources that young people can draw on and the opportunities that they have access to, we can never know exactly how the future will unfold. Their lives will change in ways that neither we, nor they, have anticipated. Henderson *et al*, 2007:165

This Chapter is divided into two sections. In the first, I draw the five separate case study stories to a close, initially by presenting the young people's retrospective views of their schooling, and then by forecasting their possible futures. In the second section I draw the story of identity to a close by rounding off three strands of this narrative: a critique of determinist approaches to the study of childhood and adolescence; a value for the capacity to create a self; and a recognition of the importance of relational awareness based on the social nature of the self.

Ending the stories: looking back and looking ahead
Looking back: What is the point of school?

Before I leave the stories of Martin, Shelley, Simon, Jayne and Liam, I draw together the remarks they made about their school careers and their reflections about what it had meant for them. There is a thin but rich seam of research on children's personal views of school, their beliefs about the purposes of schooling and their ways of imagining ideal schools (for example Burke and Grosvenor, 2003). This is linked to the wider and rapidly growing literature on consultation with pupils, pupil voice and pupil democracy, touched on in Chapter 1 (and see Alexander, 2010, for recent overview). A particularly valuable contribution to this literature can be made by young people at the point of transition from school, as their retrospective view of their school experience is fresh in their minds. The wisdom of young adults speaking from this vantage point is an untapped resource for educational policy makers and practitioners. During my final conversations with the five young people I tried to establish how they valued school, what they considered to be the point of schooling, whether they felt school could be improved for the pupils and, if so, what their ideal school would be.

In line with other research findings (Robinson and Fielding, 2010, cited in Alexander, 2010) school was valued as a key site for making friends. For example, Martin said:

> Friendship. I think that's the main drive for school, isn't it? To get up every morning and see your friends.

This is a value that teachers and policy makers need to take to heart if we are to increase children's 'liking of school', an item in which UK children scored badly compared with other countries in the UNICEF overview of child wellbeing. It is a research finding that can help teachers to create a positive learning environment and has implications for the organisation of groups in schools (Pollard, 2008).

Other attempts by the five young people to articulate the purpose of school emphasised the extrinsic rewards for learning, the benefits that would be reaped in later life through employability or higher education. As Simon put it: 'Go to learn. Get grades for a job', and Shelley: 'Guides them [pupils] along a footpath and to go into higher education and guide them into that'. This assumption about the purposes of schooling is consistent with research on children's values for school (Alexander, 2010). The assumptions of the young people about what schooling is for reflect the wider societal values for children and childhood that were discussed in Chapter 1. Their ideas emphasise the idea of schooling as first and foremost an investment in adulthood, as something that contributes to their future, rather than their present, wellbeing.

Martin, however, was cynical about this instrumental approach to school. He was particularly critical of changes in his school made by the new head teacher. He characterised these changes in an interesting way, implicitly criticising the performance driven nature of the school and challenging its lack of purpose. His analysis echoes Rogoff's discussion of modern western education as a form of 'assembly-line instruction' (2003):

> It is a different school. It's more like, we always say it's more like a factory now. You pop a pupil in and they come out with some grades at the end of it ... I don't think that's the aim, I don't really know what the aim is.

Some researchers have tried to get children to describe their ideal school. For example Burke and Grosvenor (2003) followed up a fascinating competition called 'The School I'd Like', a repeat of a much earlier, 1960s, request for children to portray their ideal schools, through the mediums of creative writing and art work (Blishen, 1969). I asked the young people how their ideal school might resemble or differ from their recent school. Their views were interesting and reflected some of the characteristics and experiences described earlier. Simon's enjoyment of sport influenced his answers: 'In the mornings they should have sport for a couple of hours'. Then, linking his value for physical sport to his understandable interest in self protection: 'They should have self defence. They should get a boxing ring so if owt happens in school you'll know what to do'. Shelley felt schools could be improved by having more school trips and by 'abolishing break times', a view that was contradicted by Simon who felt, 'They should have longer break times. Rest your brain'.

Researchers find it difficult to get children to see beyond the familiarity and taken-for-granted nature of school to imagine how it might be different. Martin, as we saw, claims not to see the purpose of schooling but does not feel he would want major changes: 'I would change a lot of things but they're only little things [hmm], I guess. Nothing major I wouldn't change'. His words echo the findings of Ruddock and Flutter (2000), who tell us that 'pupils are often ready to comment directly on 'bits and pieces' of the curriculum ... but for the most part pupils have little overall sense of how differently learning *might* be structured and handled' (p75). Martin made an interesting implied criticism of the curriculum:

> There's some things that I don't quite get about school, such as subjects and stuff. It's great that they, that you have a choice of what you want to do at GCSE, but sometimes I don't see why they make you do some subjects [especially when this is] stuff that you get in life already.

171

Martin's comments about his lack of understanding of the aims of school are in line with his inability to 'get' the school curriculum. In both cases he attributes the failure to his own lack of understanding rather than to the school system, although he does imply that educational purposes should be more transparent. His 'factory' comment is more directly critical, placing the blame on the head teacher. Martin was the most articulate of the five children in his reflections on school and, interestingly, the most critical.

Looking ahead

I would have liked to end my five stories with the words 'so they all lived happily ever after' but this study has taught me to expect the unlikely and to mistrust simple predictions. Inevitably though, I find that I do make guesses about the futures of these five individuals, particularly their more immediate futures, informed mainly by my last conversations with them.

Martin, I imagine, is likely to get into a university to study information technology, the subject preference he identified when we last spoke, and to enjoy life as a student. His emotional literacy, faith in his authentic self, and his established choice about his sexuality are likely to stand him in good stead as he enters adult life. In addition he has the great advantage of parental financial wealth to support him during his early adulthood.

This is not quite the case for Shelley. Whilst her enthusiasm and determination to get into higher education will probably take her into a university course in performance arts or drama, I wouldn't be surprised to find her living closer to home than her intended, costly, destination of London.

Simon's poor school outcomes and lack of educational qualifications (one GCSE in Art) will be a handicap as he embarks on adult life. However, this may be offset by the strong emotional support of his family and perhaps too by their social capital in the form of good local contacts and potential employers. During our last conversation he told me he had already gained some work experience at a local garage, a form of work that harnessed his longstanding interest in cars and that could act as a springboard for further employment opportunities.

I can imagine various possible scenarios for Jayne. Her willingness to please might bring about promotion from her work as room attendant in the hotel industry or she might move into clothing retail, an idea she mentioned when we last spoke. I wonder how much she will be influenced by her family as a reference group, especially her sisters, whose early adult lives were dominated by motherhood. Might she follow suit?

Liam commences his adult life in the most disadvantaged position of the five. He has no educational qualifications and a residual bitterness about his schooling. He lives in an area of high unemployment and high crime amongst his local peers. Whilst his mother does her best to provide a loving family home she has little in the way of social or material capital to support him.

I can only guess how Martin, Shelley, Simon, Jayne and Liam will live out their adult lives. My uncertainty is compounded by the future global uncertainties as the climate changes and societies change with it.

The story of identity

Finally, there is the story of identity to close. The three narrative strands that I draw together are: a critique of infant determinism, developed through the longitudinal nature of the study; a value for the capacity to create a self; and recognition of the social nature of the self and the importance of relational awareness.

How greatly do the early years of childhood determine later developmental outcomes?

This is a question that has been woven throughout the pages of this book, and is the specific focus of Chapters 3 and 4. It was particularly important in evaluating the quality and lasting importance of each child's induction into formal schooling. External pressures on teachers, especially those created by a performance ethos which values measurable outcomes in tests, diverts teachers from the activities that enhance their overall knowledge and understanding of their pupils such as talking to, playing with, observing and listening to them, and developing two-way communication with their families. Looking across the initial period of the five stories I am struck by the inadequacy of some of the judgements expressed about the children by early years teachers, especially about Martin, Shelley and Liam. These cases point to the need for teachers to access fuller knowledge of individual pupils based on evidence and to develop opportunities to work more closely and sympathetically with parents.

Criticism of the children's introduction to school leads to discussion of the long term implications if the school start proves disadvantageous – a question that is considered in the story of Shelley. Her difficult start at school did not appear to have left a lasting legacy: she was a well motivated student at secondary school. With hindsight, it is clear that the important factor was that her second year teacher was not unduly influenced by her Reception class teacher, and that her parents maintained their faith in her ability to settle into school. Shelley was lucky: it could have been different.

In Chapter 2, I discussed what has been termed the 'myth of infant determinism' (Guldberg, 2009), that is the dominant and pervasive assumption embedded in much developmental psychology, that significant early experiences decisively effect later development. The detailed nature of qualitative longitudinal research shines a light on this narrow approach to understanding the human lifespan and reveals instead complexity and unpredictability. It shows that life does not unfold in predictable pathways set by early experiences. For example, Jayne's trajectory of growing self confidence fell apart when she left the familiar world of school behind. Martin's coming out was a surprise, as was his revelation about his 'real' Dad. Similarly I could not have anticipated the attack on Simon and the impact it had on him. The unforeseen outcomes in the lives portrayed here, the surprising twists and turns of their childhood pathways, challenge causal explanations of human development. The mix of factors that influence later outcomes are many and complex, and over the course of the study, the one thing that has remained certain about these children's lives is their unpredictability.

However, this line of argument is also problematic when thinking about what this might mean for social and educational policy for children and young people. The critique of infant determinism tends to suggest that policy interventions in early childhood, such as attempts to counteract aspects of social deprivation, are likely to be swept away by the fickle hand of fortune. It implies that there is no point in large scale interventions such as Sure Start that attempt to compensate for early disadvantage. It implies, at the level of the individual, that insensitive teaching or parenting may not matter in the long run, and that a pupil who is turned off school because they start before they are ready will re-cover their motivation. So it can sound like an argument for policy to bury its head in the sand.

The work of researchers such as Rutter and Tizard shows us that many individuals are capable of reversing a pathway of disadvantage because they are resilient. Yet many individuals are vulnerable to a cycle of com-pounding disadvantages and do not have the forms of interpersonal and intrapersonal advantages that nourish resilience. This means that early interventions, whether on a large scale or tailored to individuals, are vital in the early years of childhood in order to create equality of opportunity and access to beneficial cycles of advantage. Early inter-vention on a widespread basis, or at individual level, is a protective buffer and can minimise risk.

A value for the capacity to construct identity

Do we really have such a thing as a self? Do we need one? In what circumstances? Could we do without one? I posed these questions in Chapter 3, drawing on various theorists who have discussed identity. In Chapter 4, I focused on its development during childhood and adoles-cence and considered theorists such as Erikson and Harter, who both portray adolescence as a phase of life in which there is a need to resolve identity issues, especially if there is conflict or identity dissonance be-tween different selves. These issues guided my interest in these five chil-dren with regard to their articulation of identity. I wanted to know to what extent these young people actually engaged in making statements about self, and in what circumstances, and whether such statements would indicate an underlying model of a consistent authentic identity, building on repeated characteristics over time.

So what did I find? Did these young people produce statements about self? My research deliberately used a whole raft of strategies designed to prompt such statements, and the children were co-operative and tried their best to answer my often difficult questions. Consequently they all made many 'self' statements throughout the study. I have no way of knowing whether any of the self descriptions they produced in con-versation with me were representative of ideas they were also articulat-

175

ing within other social contexts and with others in their lives. Although I had no way of knowing how typical such statements were, I could sometimes make guesses, based on the manner of the response. For example, Martin responded quickly and readily when asked to imagine how various others in his life might see him, whereas Liam struggled to respond. But this does not mean that Martin had a stronger sense of self, or that Liam was lacking a self. It means that Martin was simply more accustomed than Liam to the kind of self reflection I was inviting. So, yes, these children produced a lot of evidence of self construction throughout the study in response to my promptings: we were co-constructing their identity within the context of the interview.

In Chapter 3, the difference was discussed between the theory of identity that, chameleon-like, portrays the self as ever-changing according to its surrounding social context, and the theory that a consistent, authentic self is carried around like a snail shell through all social contexts. I wondered whether the children would reflect this snail shell idea of consistency over time, whether or not it would be something that mattered to them. Would they, like the young people discussed by Harter (1999), agonise over who they 'really are'?

There were occasions when the self was glimpsed without prompting. For example, when Simon at the age of seventeen compared himself with his friends, he recognised how he remains 'the same old self', whereas his friends, 'click' and 'change' to accommodate to each other, influenced by their peer group. His reference to the 'same old self' revealed Simon's value for an authenticity of self and an implicit criticism of his friends' chameleon-like behaviour. When Jayne admitted to feeling 'more myself' in the context of home compared with school she was also voicing, momentarily, an implicit idea of an authentic self. This entrenched Western model of self popped into our conversations, especially when the young people reached seventeen, revealing the dominance of this taken-for-granted model of self.

Could we do without a self? The stories confirm Erikson's linkage of identity and wellbeing. It is at times of vulnerability, especially social vulnerability, that the need for self is activated. Simon's story yields a clear example, when he spoke of strengthening himself literally and figuratively after hitting the low point at the fateful moment when he was attacked. We have other examples too. Jayne's insecurities focused especially on a feeling during her transition into the adult world of work of not knowing what she wanted to do or be. A contrary example, that also shows the value of self, can be seen in Martin's resilience to the traumatic news of his newly discovered biological father. His capacity for self awareness enabled him to cope with potentially difficult emotional experiences provoked through this discovery. The construction of self is especially necessary at times of transition, or following emotionally difficult times, for bolstering the self when it has become fragile.

My witnessing of part of these children's lives, together with sociological and psychological theories about identity, lead me to conclude that a sense of self is a resource for coping and managing our social experiences. Coping has both an emotional dimension, as the examples above suggest, and a cognitive, categorising dimension. Identity forms the blinkers through which we experience the world as we simultaneously distil aspects that are self-relevant and filter out aspects that are self-irrelevant. So it is a necessity for managing and controlling our lives, a vital aspect of our mental health and wellbeing. This makes it essential that policy addresses the issue of how we can help identity along, and that we are more specific about the ways we conceptualise identity. This is especially true when theories of identity are applied when developing social policy, for example when articulating educational purposes and pedagogies.

Should we try to strengthen a sense of self?

The notion of a 'strong sense of self' as an end point of socio-emotional aspects of education (e.g. Alexander, 2010; Sure Start, 2005) is problematic. We need to be wary of strategies that encourage an over rigid sense of self, since a strong sense of self can inhibit learning and change (Warin and Muldoon, 2009). As Dweck has pointed out (2000) with regard to the disadvantages of a fixed 'entity' set of beliefs about self, an over rigid identity inhibits an openness to change and learning. This begins to sound paradoxical. Surely if identity is crucial to wellbeing and learning then it must be beneficial to strengthen it?

So there is a paradox surrounding the value of identity and how it is best translated into policy. Its significance for wellbeing and learning does not mean we need to have more of it or that it needs to be strengthened. Interventions in identity construction should not be aimed at strengthening the self. They should be aimed instead at strengthening a person's capacity to create self, their capacity to expand and differentiate identity into a sophisticated, nuanced story. Interventions need to help people to narrate a story that can encompass disparate self elements, synthesise identity dissonance, and incorporate sub-plots. The metaphor of story-telling used here seems to allow this fluidity and complexity as well as emphasising the language demands, and emotional literacy, implicit in identity construction. In other words, it is the capacity for self narration that appears to be so advantageous.

The capacity for telling a story of self gives us a kind of 'identity capital', a stock of resources that is readily available when we require them. My analysis of the data, together with my new insights into some of the theoretical tensions relating to identity construction, have produced the concept of identity capital as a conceptual hook on which to hang some key conclusions. It pre-supposes that those who have developed this capacity are at an advantage.

A recognition of the social nature of self

Another narrative strand has concerned the social nature of identity. The interdependent nature of individual processes and group processes was explored in Chapter 3. Our understanding about individual psychology will deepen when we acknowledge the importance of the social context around the individual. Similarly, we will understand groups and societies better when we understand more about the influence of the individuals who make them up. Theorists have managed to maintain a perspective that includes a simultaneous and equal focus on the individual and the social, amongst them Asch, Mead, Vygotsy and Giddens. They have crossed the boundaries between the disciplines of sociology and psychology, recognising the reciprocity between them, and discovering the need for sociologists and psychologists to work together. The social psychologist Asch (1952:285), who studied group processes, insisted that we need to understand the reality of 'individual and group'. He described these as 'the two permanent poles of all social processes'.

This is easier said than done. In designing and carrying out the study presented in this book, I tried to maintain a perspective on both the individual and their social context, at one and the same time. However, calling the book 'Stories of Self' emphasises the individual process of self making and perhaps under-emphasises the social context.

Self awareness or relational awareness?

Terminology is important to how we conceptualise goals in social policy and how we separate out academic disciplines and their attendant theories and bodies of knowledge. The term 'relational awareness' is a way of trying to express the interdependence between a value for developing insight into self and developing insight into others. But it is not a term that trips easily off the tongue. Perhaps we need to emphasise terms such as empathy and social awareness when conceptualising the goals of wellbeing and the educational and wider social policies that can best serve them. Both these terms swing more to the social pole and underplay the individual pole. This may be a necessary counterbalance to our recent emphasis on individual growth and the individualistic concept of self esteem.

In The Cambridge Primary Review (Alexander, 2010) the twelve aims presented for primary education include aims under the heading 'The individual' and 'Self, others, and the wider world'. The latter category highlights the word 'reciprocity' and also respect for both self and others. The statement of aims gives equal weight to goals focused on the individual and goals, focused on 'others', together with a recognition of the reciprocity between such goals. This marks a positive development away from an over emphasis on individualism.

A growing critique of individualism

Layard (2005) claims that the twentieth century saw the demise of widely accepted religious and ethical conceptions of morality. 'Into the void', he says, 'stepped the non-philosophy of rampant individualism'. He maintains:

> At its best this individualism offered 'self realisation'. But that gospel failed. It did not increase happiness, because it made each individual too anxious about what he could get for himself. (p5)

This argument also underpins the findings of *The Good Childhood Inquiry* conducted by Layard and Dunn (2009). A key message of their report is that excessive individualism in the wider society creates a competitive culture in which adults strive for independent personal success at the expense of family life and concern for dependent children. These authors argue that children's wellbeing will be improved when we have a created an ethic in which we care more for each other. The next and final Chapter considers how this purpose, and the relational awareness that underpins it, might be translated into education policy.

12

So what?
What can education policy do?

Longitudinal research can highlight the range of factors that impact on people's lives ... it can thus better inform policy-making. Holland *et al*, 2006: 25

The value of identity construction, and the extent to which schools can and should provide for this, raises important questions about the aims of education and the sort of society we want to live in. Academics are drawing attention to the lack of explicit educational purpose in current schooling (Hayward *et al*, 2005; McLaughlin, 2005; Alexander, 2010; Pollard, 2009). McLaughlin emphasises that personal and emotional development must be at the heart of all re-examination of the purposes of education.

Opportunities and resources for developing the capacity to tell a story of self

What school based opportunities contributed to these stories of self told by Martin, Shelley, Simon, Jayne and Liam? What worked for them? What failed? How far do their school careers reflect wider policy, and especially policies concerned with the development of intrapersonal resources, such as the capacity for constructing self, and for interpersonal resources such as relational awareness?

The five young people attended school during a phase of educational policy in the UK, under New Labour, in which education was dominated by a political agenda emphasising performance goals and educational standards. At secondary school they all received statutory Personal, Social and Health Education (PSHE) lessons, arguably a context for pupils to develop identity capital. But PHSE lessons offered little information about such opportunities. Martin and Shelley both reported that their relationships with their PSHE teachers were good because they could talk with them, a point discussed below. However, they received little explicit teaching of interpersonal and intrapersonal skills. None of the children participated in 'circle time', a practice for developing pro-social skills inspired by the work of Mosley (1996), and now more widespread in primary schools than it was when they were primary school age. They did not benefit from the explicit social and emotional skills training that informs initiatives such as SEAL (Social and Emotional Aspects of Learning). There was one interesting and extremely positive exception: Jayne's school provided a 'little club thing – every Monday – for helping me to be confident'.

Educational purposes, wellbeing and the creation of identity capital

At the time of writing something of a sea-change is occurring: interpersonal and intrapersonal educational aims and values are becoming a priority in UK education policy, linked to the increasing emphasis on wellbeing. Weare (2004) points out the usefulness of the term 'wellbeing' because it is 'a generic, broad and encompassing term which is, on the whole, uncontroversial and acceptable to a wide range of educational, social care and health related environments' (p8). Her analysis explains why the term has become so prevalent, especially in UK policy discourses, since the *Every Child Matters* green paper (2003) and the follow-up legislation. This requires conceptualising the child-oriented goals that are the end point of interprofessional collaboration. It can therefore be seen to operate as a kind of policy glue, a way of sticking together the varied professional goals of those who work with children and young people.

Weare also points out the 'extraordinary pace' of work on emotional literacy, and related concepts such as emotional intelligence, emotional and social competence, and positive mental health. Foley (2008) claims that 'Social issues, including the wellbeing of children, have replaced economic issues at the top of the political agenda' (p1). Relating closely to 'wellbeing', Alexander (2004a and 2004b) discusses the appearance of the term 'enjoyment' in the UK's 2003 *Excellence and Enjoyment: a strategy for Primary Schools*, a word that also features in *Every Child Matters* (2003), where 'enjoying and achieving' are linked in the third of the ECM outcomes. So there is much evidence of lip service to the goal of wellbeing.

Another goal is emotional literacy, in which the development of self understanding and the creation of identity capital are seen to be vital. But this view may be over-optimistic, and indeed Ball (2008) dismisses these claims. He points to the ongoing dominance of underlying economic priorities as undercutting these goals. Alexander (2010) similarly suggests that 'enjoyment' is used rhetorically and, like Ball, argues that the focus of English education policy remains on assessment and standards. Are the goals of wellbeing, emotional literacy and enjoyment really translated into living policy and educational intervention in the UK and globally? What is the role of Citizenship, SEAL, Personalised Learning and anti-bullying strategies?

In the last decade a number of policy initiatives have attempted to place goals of social understanding and self understanding higher up the educational agenda. For example Citizenship Education, introduced in England and Wales in the late nineties, seemed to promise delivery of these goals, particularly emphasising interpersonal skills. However, as McLaughlin (2005) has pointed out, Citizenship education tried to fulfil too many political and educational goals all at once. In reality it has now become embedded in the History and PSHE curricula.

A value for self awareness and closely related concepts is built into the aims of the programme of social and emotional aspects of learning (SEAL) that was introduced, initially in English primary schools, in 2005 and now adopted by many secondary schools. The main aim of the SEAL initiative has been to develop the emotional intelligence of children. It draws on the work of Goleman (1991), who defined emotional intelligence as the capacity for recognising one's own feelings and those of others, and for managing emotions in our social relationships as well as in ourselves. Of specific relevance to the building of identity, the SEAL curriculum materials include a thematic unit entitled 'Good to be me' which encourages pupils to think about what is 'special' about them and how they are different to others.

The term 'personalised learning' appeared in 2004 in government speeches on education, and was to be based on a 'sound knowledge and understanding of every child's needs' (Pollard and James, 2004). At first glance it seems to have the potential to focus on the learning needs of the individual and offer teaching to match, commensurate with the wishful thinking of the Every Child Matters agenda (Hartley, 2007). The purposes underlying this concept appear closely linked to a holistic approach in education policy to children's overall wellbeing.

The current tide of interest in social and emotional aspects of learning is global. Amongst the leading countries in identifying the importance of promoting wellbeing in education is Australia. The primary aim of their 'Kids Matter' initiative is to improve the wellbeing and mental health of pupils in primary school. This initiative attempts to promote emotional intelligence by encouraging emotional control, self aware-ness and, specifically, resilience to situations which may cause emo-tional distress, such as loss and change.

Bullying has had an enormously high profile during the last ten years. Some commentators, for example Gill (2007), suggest that we are in the grip of a moral panic about it. As a consequence of its high profile in the media, and perhaps also through forums in which children and young people themselves express their anxieties about bullying, anti-bullying policies and initiatives have been established in many countries. Valu-able initiatives have been spawned through this concern, such as buddy schemes and peer counselling, in which intrapersonal and inter-personal skills have a strong and explicit presence.

The co-existence of pro-social goals and economically driven performance goals

According to Shuayb and O'Donnell (2008) however, the first years of the 21st century have reflected a dual set of educational aims and values. These authors identify the continuation of economic and politi-cally influenced performance goals lurking alongside a focus on chil-dren's social and emotional wellbeing. These make uncomfortable bed-fellows. The policy initiatives for enhancing personal qualities are undercut by the stronger policy drive for economic competition. Ball (2008) makes this point clearly in his analysis of education in the UK over the last twenty years:

The social and economic purposes of education have been collapsed into a single, overriding emphasis on policy making for economic competitiveness and an increasing neglect or sidelining (other than in rhetoric) of the social purposes of education. (p11-12)

Educational performance dominates educational policy making at every level, creating a culture that is driven by league tables. Pupils' performances in the classroom are compared. In the educational marketplace, the performance of schools is compared. In the global marketplace the school performance of countries is compared. The dominant paradigm is that 'what matters is measured' and, by implication, 'what cannot be measured does not matter' (Shuayb and O'Donnell, 2008). In this climate of competition, teachers are drawn, often against their better judgment, into a focus on performance outcomes. It is extremely challenging to measure social and emotional aspects of education and draw comparisons between pupils, schools and countries.

Both SEAL and 'personalisation' have been criticised on grounds of overemphasis on individualism. For example, Ball (2008) links personalisation to a policy emphasis on individualism, the 'imperative of self determination' which he sees, not only in education policy but in the raft of public service policies. He asserts, quoting Blair (2002), that these policies are designed to steer individuals to 'make something of their lives and use their ability and potential to the full' (p204), but that this aim, though apparently innocuous, does not take account of the relational aspects of human existence and fulfilment. This aim brings to mind the 'self actualising' goals of humanist identity theorists such as Maslow (1954), who fail to recognise that most people exist in social contexts of interdependence, where individual goals of self fulfilment are complicated by co-existence with others. Hartley (2007) argues that the concept of personalised learning does not suggest any radical changes to pedagogy or to the curriculum, but provides, instead, a seductive rhetoric of individual learning needs driven by marketing theory. He maintains that: 'personalisation takes the marketisation of education a stage further, by placing it at the very heart of the pedagogical process' (p630).

Threats and opportunities

The good news then is that current policy noises about child wellbeing and personalised learning offer a context in which children are likely to have more opportunities in school to develop a language and practice of self narration, to build identity capital. In the UK, fruitful ways ahead lie in the emphasis on enjoyment and wellbeing and the introduction of SEAL, which goes beyond rhetoric since it is now well resourced. The gradual shift to recognising the integration of child-focused goals and the joining up of services means there is a more holistic approach to goals concerning the development of overall wellbeing rather than only narrowly defined scholastic achievement. These developments provide grounds for optimism about the educational aims that are the concern of this book.

However, the bad news is that there are several obstacles to the implementation of policies and initiatives. One possible obstacle may lie in an interpretation of social and emotional aspects of learning as a fostering of individualism. Efforts to develop a 'strong self' and to 'personalise' learning, so that each child is pursuing their own isolated pathway could create a climate of individualism and increase competition.

A second threat lies in locating the means of creating opportunities in the school curriculum for the development of interpersonal and intrapersonal learning. This generates unproductive debates about curriculum overcrowding and battles over the prioritisation of discrete school subject disciplines. Media discussion of the government's Rose report (2009) and the simultaneous Cambridge Primary Review of Education (Alexander, 2010) has often been about curriculum time at the expense of deeper questions about the moral purposes of education. We need to recognise that school based opportunities to build identity capital will not emerge from additional curriculum time, but will only thrive within a whole-school approach. Weare (2004) argues that the development of emotional literacy in a school setting will only come about through a whole-school approach that incorporates all aspects of school life, for example assemblies, communication with parents, relationships between staff and between pupils and staff. A shift from a discussion of curriculum to an emphasis on pedagogy would be a fruitful way forward since pedagogy incorporates the all-important aspect of relationships with teachers.

The importance of relationships with teachers

The five school trajectories analysed here highlight how pupils need to have positive relationships with teachers. Such relationships influenced how, when and where the children's beliefs about self were constructed. For example Jayne, who experienced some shyness and anxieties at her primary school, had particularly positive relationships with teachers in her secondary school, whom she described as 'friends and 'really nice', and with whom she felt able to talk during lunch hour. When she was chosen to be Head Girl (in year 11, at age fifteen), knowing that she was strongly valued by staff was confirmed. Her dip in confidence on leaving school can be attributed to her loss of this strong source of approval and affirmation. Martin's trust of a particular teacher led him to disclose his recently established gay sexuality. This seemed especially important at a time in his life when his relationships with his parents were beginning to be strained since his discovery about his father.

However, not all the children had positive and supportive relationships with teachers, in which they could articulate 'self'. Liam's relationships with teachers were poor and for Simon they were inadequate. Neither boy could be reintegrated into secondary school after lengthy periods of absenteeism. The stories also revealed several cases of inadequate teacher/pupil relationships in the early years of primary school. The five stories show clearly that good relationships with teachers enable opportunities for identity capital to be created.

Positive teacher/pupil relationships may be more important in promoting interpersonal and intrapersonal capacities than curriculum, based opportunities. Many taken-for-granted practices need to be radically rethought. If policy makers and practitioners focus their attention on adding to the curriculum they are unlikely to promote these personal capacities. If, instead, they concentrate on developing the art and science of pedagogy, as recommended by Pollard (2010) among others, they will create a more fertile ground for realising pro-social goals.

The hegemony of economic goals, however, is likely to be a major obstacle to helping children to build identity. According to Shuayb and O'Donnell (2008) and Ball (2008), the two goals which are currently the focus of school policy discourse are at odds. The ongoing influence of performance goals is fundamentally incompatible with the philosophies of personalised teaching. Policy initiatives aimed at fulfilling intrapersonal and interpersonal educational goals are likely to lose out to the economic pressures to produce measurable educational outcomes. The mantra remains 'what matters is measured' and 'what cannot be measured does not matter'. We begin by trying to measure what we value but end up valuing only that which can be measured.

Conclusion

This book has argued for social and emotional goals to be given higher value and status within education. This includes attributing value for the capacity to tell a story of self as part of a broader relational awareness. Yet unless we raise their status, such goals will only be the poor relations of measurable educational outcomes. So how do we move beyond this *impasse*? If measurement is so vital, we need to develop highly sophisticated methods for assessing social and emotional progress, for example through triangulating teacher assessments. The challenge facing educational practitioners and policy-makers today is to raise the status within education of the goal of developing each pupil's relational intelligence, social awareness and understanding, and compassion.

Appendix 1
Background information to the stories of Martin, Shelley, Simon, Jayne and Liam

Martin (Chapter 6)
Family composition. Martin lived with his mother Karen, and his father, Andrew. During his adolescence Martin found out that Andrew was not his biological father and he traced his biological father Terry. Martin's sister Rachel was born when he was five. He had two older siblings, a half-brother and half-sister (Andrew's children) who were approximately seven and eight years older than him, and who lived in Martin's family for some of the time during most of his childhood and primary school years. His older half-brother was still living in the family home when Martin was interviewed at the age of 17.

Ethnic identity. White British.

Parental employment. Both Karen and Andrew worked full time throughout the duration of the study. Andrew was a bank manger and Karen held various middle management positions in a bank.

Housing. Own house. When the study began Karen and Andrew lived in a newly built executive housing estate in a quiet cul-de-sac on the outskirts of town. Towards the end of Martin's primary schooling the family moved to a larger house close to the old one.

Schooling
Nursery/Pre-school. Hazel Grove. Private.
Primary school. Bath Square. Urban primary, middle sized, with a small proportion of Asian Indian children.
Secondary school. St Stephen's. Middle size, 11 – 18, Church of England school. Martin remained in the school from age 11 to the end of 6th form at age 18.

Shelley (Chapter 7)
Family composition. Shelley lived with her mother Tess, father Brian and her older half-brother Patrick, ten years her senior. Patrick was Tess's son from her first marriage.

Ethnic identity. White British.

Parental employment. Tess and Brian were both unemployed at the start of study. Brian had been in the building trade but ceased work following an accident and was in receipt of a disability allowance. Tess undertook some part time work in the home, as a seamstress. At the time Shelley left her secondary school for a college of further education, Tess and Brian moved to a new home and started their own business in a village some twenty miles away.

Housing. Own house. Small end terrace house in a council estate.

Schooling
Nursery/Pre-school. St. Oswald's, a pre-school playgroup run by the local church. Shelley attended only a few sessions, two mornings a week, in the summer before she started school.
Primary school. Bridge View Primary School. Large urban primary serving large council estate (also attended by Liam).
Secondary school. Forest Hill High School. Large urban comprehensive, 11-16 (also attended by Liam).

Simon (Chapter 8)

Family composition. Simon lived with his mother, Kath, father, Paul, older brother Garry and younger sister Laura who was a baby at the start of the study. Another brother, Ryan, was born when Simon was six.

Ethnic identity. White British.

Parental employment: Paul was a porter at the university at the start of the study and then moved into a self employed DIY and decorating job. Kath was unemployed throughout the study.

Housing. The house was a terrace house, owned by Paul and Kath. It was small given the increasing size of the family. The family lived there throughout the study.

Schooling
Nursery/Pre-school. Brompton nursery. Purpose built nursery attached to Brompton Primary School (also attended by Jayne).
Primary school. Brompton Primary School. Urban primary school, of medium size, in Simon's immediate neighbourhood, within easy walking distance (also attended by Jayne).
Secondary school. St Mary's. Large Catholic comprehensive, (11- 18), very close to his home.

Jayne (Chapter 9)

Family composition. Jayne lived with her mother Helen, father Kevin and two older sisters, Vicky and Gina, who were close in age to each other and were at secondary school at the start of the study. Kevin was considerably older than Helen and was in poor health throughout the study. By the time Jayne was seventeen both her sisters had moved into their own homes with young families of their own and Jayne spent time with her young nieces.

Ethnic identity. White British.

Parental employment. Both parents were unemployed at start of study. Helen was employed as care worker during Jayne's secondary school years.

Housing. Council house.

Schooling
Nursery/Pre-school. Brompton nursery. Purpose built nursery attached to Brompton Primary School (also attended by Simon).
Primary school. Brompton Primary School. Urban primary school, of medium size, fairly close to her home (also attended by Simon).
Secondary school attended. Northend High School. Small, 11 – 16, urban comprehensive.

Liam (Chapter 10)

Family composition. At the start of the study Liam lived with his mother Donna and her parents. His 'real' Dad was known to him but never visited. He spent a lot of his time with his granddad and this remained a close relationship throughout the period of the study. Towards the end of his primary schooling Donna was re-partnered with Jason and a new young sister, Kimberley, was born. Jason left the family during Liam's early years at secondary school. After this, Donna, Liam and Kimberly lived together as a stable family unit.

Ethnic identity. White British

Parental employment. Donna was unemployed throughout study. She suffered from depression and received disability benefit.

Housing. At the start of the study Donna and Liam lived with his grandparents in their small terrace council house that was conveniently situated next door to the Osborne Centre (see below). Seven years later he had moved into a council housing estate on the edge of the town, with Donna, Kimberley and Jason. When Jason left, Donna was housed in a caravan park for several months, followed by a second temporary home in another caravan park and finally in a council house on the Banks housing estate where the family remained.

Schooling
Nursery/Pre-school. The Osborne Centre. Purpose built Social Services nursery.
Primary school. Bridge View Primary School. Large urban primary serving large council estate (also attended by Shelley).
Secondary school. Forest Hill High School. Large urban comprehensive, 11-16, (also attended by Shelley).
Pupil Referral Unit. Cragside.

Appendix 2
Figurative diagram used with the children at age 12/13

References

Alderson, P (1995) *Listening to Children: Children, ethics and social research.* Barkingside: Barnardo's

Aldridge, J and Becker, S (2003) *Children Caring for Parents with Mental Illness. Perspectives of young carers, parents and professionals.* Bristol: Policy Press

Alexander, R J (2004a) Excellence, Enjoyment and Personalised Learning: a true foundation for choice? *Education Review,* 18(1) p15-33

Alexander, R J (2004b) Still no pedagogy? Principle, pragmatism, and compliance in primary education. *Cambridge Journal of Education* 34 (1) p7-33

Alexander, R J (ed) (2010) *Children, their World, their Education. Final report and recommendations of the Cambridge Primary Review.* Abingdon: Routledge

Anning, A (2005) Investigating the impact of working in integrated service delivery settings in the UK on early years practitioners' beliefs and practices. *Journal of Early Childhood Research* 3: p19-50

Apted, M (1964, *continuing*) The *Up series.* TV documentaries. Five Disk Collectors edtn. DVD

Aries, P (1973) Centuries of Childhood: A social history of family life. Harmondsworth: Penguin

Asch, S E (1952) *Social Psychology.* Englewood Cliffs, NJ: Prentice Hall

Atkinson, P (1990) *The Ethnographic Imagination: textual construction of reality.* London and NY: Routledge

Ball, S J (2008) *The Education Debate: Policy and politics in the 21st Century.* Bristol: Policy Press

Barnes, D (1976) *From Communication to Curriculum.* Harmondsworth: Penguin Education

Baron-Cohen, S (1991) Precursors to a theory of mind: Understanding attention in others. In Whiten, A (ed) *Natural theories of mind: evolution, development and simulation of everyday mindreading.* Oxford: Basil Blackwell

Barrett, H (2006) *Attachment and the Perils of Parenting. A commentary and a critique.* London: National Family and Parenting Institute

195

Bauman, Z (2001) *The Individualized Society*. Cambridge: Polity Press

Baumeister, R F (1986) *Identity, Cultural Change and the Struggle for the Self*. Oxford: Oxford University Press

Baumeister, R F, Campbell, J D, Krueger, J I and Vohs, K D (2003) Does high self-esteem cause better performance, interpersonal success, happiness or healthier life-styles? *Psychological Science in the Public Interest*. 4(1) p1-44

BBC/Open University (2001, *continuing*) *Child of Our Time*

Beck, U and Beck-Gernsheim, E (2002) *Individualisation*. London: Sage

Bell, J F and Daniels, S (1990) Are summer-born children disadvantaged? The birth-date effect in education. *Oxford Review of Education*.16, 1, p67-80

Benhabib, S (1992) *Situating the Self: gender, community, and postmodernism in contemporary ethics*. Cambridge: Polity Press

Bernstein, B (1971) *Class, Codes and Control. Towards a theory of educational trans-mission*. London: Paladin

Biddulph, S (2003) *Raising Boys: why boys are different – and how to help them become happy and well-balanced men*. London: Thorsons

Blishen, E (1969) *The School that I'd Like*. Penguin Education Special, Harmonds-worth: Penguin Books

Bowlby, J (1988) *A Secure Base: clinical applications of attachment theory*. London: Routledge

Bourdieu, P and Passeron, J C (1990) *Reproduction in Education, Society and Cul-ture*. London: Sage

Bradshaw, J Smith, M and Jackson, A (2007) *ESRC Seminar series. Mapping the public policy landscape. Well-being for children and young people*. Swindon: ESRC

Brannen J, Heptinstall E, Bhopal K (2000) *Connecting Children. Care and family life in later childhood*. Routledge Falmer: London.

Brice-Heath, S (1983) *Ways with Words: Language, life, and work in communities and classrooms*. New York: McGraw-Hill: Oxford University Press

British Educational Research Association (BERA) (2004) *Ethical Guidelines* http://www.bera.ac.uk/files/guidelines/ethica1.pdf (December 2009)

British Psychologial Society (BPS) (2009) *Code of Ethics and Conduct*. http://www.bps.org.uk/document-downlaod (December 2009)

Broadhead, P (2004) *Early Years Play and Learning: developing social skills and co-operation*. London: Routledge Falmer

Broadhurst, K, Grover, C, and Jamieson, J (eds) (2009) *Critical Perspectives on Safe-guarding Children*. Oxford: Wiley-Blackwell

Brooker, L (2002) *Starting School. Young children learning cultures*. Buckingham: Open University Press

Brooks, L (2006) *The Story of Childhood. Growing up in modern Britain*. London: Bloomsbury Publishing

Bruner, J (1990) *Acts of Meaning.* Cambridge, MA: Harvard University Press

Bruner, J S (1996) *The Culture of Education.* Cambridge MA: Harvard University Press

Burke, C and Grosvenor, I (2003) *The School I'd Like. Children and young people's reflections on an education for the 21st century,* London: Routledge

Burman, E (2008) *Deconstructing Developmental Psychology 2nd edition.* London and New York: Routledge.

Byrne, B M (1996) *Measuring Self Concept Across the Lifespan. Issues and Instrumentation.* Washington: American Psychological Association

Centre for Longitudinal Studies: http://www.cls.ioe.ac.uk/news.asp?section=0001000 10003&item=473 (September, 2009)

Christensen, P and James, A (2000) *Research with Children. Perspectives and Practices.* London: Routledge Falmer

Claffey, A E, Kucharski, L J and Gratz, Rene R (1994) Managing the biting child. *Early Child Development and Care.* 99 p93-101.

Coffey, A (1999) *The Ethnographic self: fieldwork and the representation of identity.* London: Sage

Coleman, J (2009) Well-being in schools: empirical measure, or politician's dream? *Oxford Review of Education. Special edition on child wellbeing in school.* 35, 3 p281-292

Collins, J (1996) *The Quiet Child.* London: Cassell

Cooley, C H (1902) *Human nature and the social order.* New York: Charles Scribner's Sons

Corsaro, W A and Molinari, L (2000) Entering and Observing in Children's Worlds: a reflection on a longitudinal ethnography of early education in Italy. In Christensen, P and James, A (eds) *Research with Children: perspectives and practices.* London: Falmer

Coté, J E (1996) Sociological perspectives on identity formation: the culture-identity link and identity capital. *Journal of Adolescence.* 19 p417-428

Cotterell, J (1996) *Social networks and social influences in adolescence.* New York: Routledge

Craig, C (2009) Well-being in schools: The curious case of the tail wagging the dog?, Centre for Confidence and Well-being, www.centreforconfidence.co.uk (October 2009)

Crozier, G (2002) Beyond the call of duty: the impact of racism on black parents' involvement in their children's education. Paper presented at ESRC Sponsored Seminar Series *Parents and Schools: Diversity, Participation and Democracy.* University East Anglia, 20th June 2001

Curtiss, S (1977) *Genie: a psycholinguistic study of a modern-day 'wild child'.* Boston: Academic Press

Daniels, S, Shorrocks-Taylor, D and Redfern, E (2000) Can Starting Summer-born Children Earlier at Infant School improve their National Curriculum Results? *Oxford Review of Education.* 26 (2) p207-220

David, T (2001) Curriculum in the Early Years. In Pugh G (ed) *Contemporary Issues in the Early Years.* London: Sage, Paul Chapman Publishing

Davies, B (1982) *Life in the Classroom and Playground,* London: Routledge and Kegan Paul

Davies, B (1987) The accomplishment of genderedness in pre-school children. In Pollard A (ed) *Children and Their Primary Schools: A New Perspective.* London: Falmer

Davies, B and Harre, R (1990) Positioning: the discursive production of selves. *Journal for the Theory of Social Behaviour.* 20 (1) p43-63

Davies, B (1989) *Frogs and Snails and Feminist Tales: pre-school children and gender.* Sydney: Allen and Unwin

Dennet, D (1991) *Consciousness Explained.* Harmondsworth: Penguin

Denscombe, M (2000) Social conditions for stress: young people's experience of doing GCSEs, *British Educational Research Journal,* 26, 3 p359 -374

DES (Department of Education and Science) (1989) *Discipline in Schools,* Report of the Committee of Enquiry chaired by Lord Elton: Her Majesty's Stationery Office

DfEE (Department for Education and Employment) (1998) *Meeting the Child Care Challenge.* Her Majesty's Stationery Office

DfES (Department for Education and Skills) (2003) *Every Child Matters,* DfES

DfES (2005) *Excellence and Enjoyment: learning and teaching in the primary years,* London: DfES

Donaldson, M (1978) *Children's Minds.* London: Collins Fontana

Draper, L and Duffy, B (2001) Working with Parents. In Pugh, G (ed) *Contemporary Issues in the Early Years.* London: Sage, Paul Chapman Publishing

Dunn, J (1988) *The Beginnings of Social Understanding.* Oxford: Blackwell

Dweck, C S (2000) *Self-Theories: Their Role in Motivation, Personality and Development.* Philadelphia: Psychology Press

Easen, P, Atkins, M, Dyson A (2000) Inter-professional collaboration and conceptualisations of practice. *Children and Society,* 14: p355-367

Edwards, A and Knight, P (1994) *Effective Early Years Education.* Buckingham: Open University Press

Ecclestone, S and Hayes, D (2008) *The Dangerous Rise of Therapeutic Education,* London: Routledge

Emerson, R, Fretz, R and Shaw, L (1995) *Writing Ethnographic Fieldnotes.* Chicago: University of Chicago Press

Emler, N (2001) *Self esteem: the costs and causes of low self worth.* York: York Publishing Services

Engler, B (2008) *Personality Theories: an introduction.* 8th edition. Belmont, California: Wadsworth.

Epstein, D (1993) *Changing Classroom Cultures: anti-racism, politics and schools.* Stoke-on-Trent: Trentham Books

Erikson, E H (1980) *Identity and the Life Cycle.* New York: Norton

Fabian, H (2002) *Children Starting School. A guide to successful transitions and transfers for teachers and assistants.* London: David Fulton

Faulkner, D (1995) Play, self and the social world. In Barnes, P (ed) *Personal, Social and Emotional Development of Children.* Oxford: Blackwell

Festinger, L (1954) A theory of social comparison processes. *Human Relations,* 7(2) p117-140

Foley, P (2008) Introduction. In J, Collins and P, Foley (eds) *Promoting Children's Wellbeing: policy and practice.* Bristol: Policy Press in association with The Open University

Foresight Project on Mental Capital and Wellbeing (July 2006 – October 2008) http://www.foresight.gov.uk/OurWork/ActiveProjects/Mental%20Capital/Welcome.asp (December, 2009)

Gardner, H (1983) *Frames of Mind: the theory of multiple intelligences.* New York: Basic Books

Gergen, K J (1991) *The Saturated Self.* New York: Basic Books

Gerhardt, S (2004) *Why Love Matters: how affection shapes a baby's brain.* Hove: Brunner-Routledge

Gewirtz, S (2001) Cloning the Blairs: New Labour's programme for the resocialisation of working class parents. *Journal of Education Policy* 16: 365-378.

Gewirtz, S (2008) Give Us a Break! A sceptical review of contemporary discourses of lifelong learning, *European Educational Research Journal,* 7 (4): p414-424

Giddens, A (1984) *The Constitution of Society. Outline of the theory of structuration.* Cambridge: Polity Press

Giddens, A (1991) *Modernity and Self-Identity: self and society in the late modern age.* Cambridge: Polity Press

Gill, T (2007) *No Fear: growing up in a risk averse society.* London: Calouste Gulbenkian Society

Glass, N (1999) Sure Start: the development of an early intervention programme for young children in the United Kingdom. *Children and Society,* 13, 4, p257-364

Goleman, D (1996) *Emotional Intelligence, Why it can matter more than IQ.* London: Bloomsbury

Goleman, D (2007) *Social Intelligence.* London: Arrow

Golombok, S (2000) *Parenting: What really counts?* London: Routledge

Goncu, A (1998) Development of Intersubjectivity in Social Pretend Play. In Woodhead M, Faulkner, D, and Littleton, K (eds) *Cultural Worlds of Early Childhood.* London and NY: Routledge

Goodson, I and Sikes, P (2001) *Life History in Educational Settings: learning from lives.* Buckingham: Open University Press

Green, S (2002) *BTEC National Early Years*. Edexcel: Nelson Thorne

Greene, S (1999) Child development: old themes, new directions. In Woodhead, M, Faulkner, D and Littleton, K (eds) *Making Sense of Social Development*. London: Routledge

Greene, S and Hogan, D (2005) *Researching Children's Experience: approaches and methods*. London: Sage.

Greenman, J (1995) Reality bites (frequently): Biting at the centre – Part 2. *Child Care Information Exchange*, 10 p65-67

Griffiths, M (1995) *Feminisms and the Self*. London: Routledge

Grimshaw, J (1986) *Feminist Philosophers: women's perspectives on philosophical positions*. Brighton: Wheatsheaf

Gudmundsdottir, S (1996) The teller, the tale and the one being told: the narrative nature of the research interview. *Curriculum Inquiry*, 26, p293-306

Guldberg, H (2009) *Reclaiming Childhood. Freedom and play in an age of fear*. London: Routledge

Hall, S and du Gay, P (1996) *Questions of Cultural Identity*. London: Sage

Hammersley, M and Atkinson P (2007) *Ethnography: principles in practice*. 3rd edition. London: Routledge

Harding, L M (2000) Supporting Families/Controlling families? Towards a Characterisation of New Labour's 'Family Policy'. Paper presented at ESRC seminar series: Postmodern Kinship, Leeds University

Harding, S (1993) Rethinking Standpoint Epistemology: What is strong objectivity? In Alcoff, L and Potter, E (eds) *Feminist Epistemologies*. New York: Routledge

Hardyment, C (1983) *Dream Babies*. Oxford: Oxford University Press

Hargreaves, D H (1967) *Social Relations in a Secondary School*. London: Routledge

Hargreaves, D H (1982) *The Challenge for the Comprehensive school; Culture, curriculum and community*. London: Routledge and Kegan Paul

Harter, S (1999) *The Construction of the Self: a developmental perspective*. NY, London: The Guilford Press

Harter, S and Pike, R (1983) *The Pictorial Scale of Perceived Competence and Social Acceptance for Young Children*. Denver: University of Denver

Hartley, D (2007) Personalisation: the emerging 'revised' code of education? *Oxford Review of Education*, 33 (5) p629 – 642

Hartup, W W (1992) Friendships and their developmental significance. In McGurk, H (ed) *Childhood Social Development*. Hillsdale: Lawrence Erlbaum Associates

Hattie, J (1992) *Self Concept*. Hillsdale. New Jersey: Lawrence Erlbaum Associates

Haywood, C, and Mac an Ghaill, M, (2003) *Men and Masculinities*. Buckingham: Open University Press

Hayward, G, Hodgson, A, Johnson, J, Oancea, A, Pring, R, Spours, K,Wilde, S and Wright, S (2005) *The Nuffield Review of 14-19 Education and Training: Annual Report, 2004-2005*. Oxford, Oxford University Press

Henderson, S, Holland, J, McGrellis, S, Sharpe, S, and Thomson, R (2007) *Inventing adulthoods; a biographical approach to youth transitions.* London: Sage

Henwood, K and Lang, I (2003) *Qualitative Research Resources: a consultation exercise with UK social scientists.* A report to the ESRC

Hey, V (1997) *The Company She Keeps: an ethnography of girls' friendships.* Buckingham: Open University Press

Holland, J, Thomson, R, Henderson, S (2006) *Qualitative Longitudinal Research: A Discussion paper.* Families and Social Capital, ESRC Research group Working Paper No 21 Swindon: ESRC

Hollway, W (1989) *Subjectivity and Method in Psychology: gender, meaning and science.* London: Sage

Hughes, M and Greenhough, P (2006) Boxes, bags and videotape: enhancing home-school communication through knowledge exchange activities, *Educational Review – Special Issue,* 58 (4) p471-487

Hunt, J (1989) *Psychoanalytic Aspects of Fieldwork.* London: Sage

Iacovou, M (2004) Life chances: childhood experiences and later outcomes. In Stewart, I and Vaitilingam, R (eds) (2004) *Seven Ages of Man and Woman.* ESRC http://www.esrcsocietytoday.ac.uk/ESRCInfoCentre/Images/seven_ages (August 2008)

Jackson C and Warin J (2000) The Importance of Gender as an Aspect of Identity at Key Transition Points in Compulsory Education, *British Educational Research Journal.* 26 (3) p375-392

Jackson, P (1968) *Life in Classrooms.* New York and London: Teachers' College Press

James, A and Prout, A (eds) (1990) *Constructing and Reconstructing Childhood.* Basingstoke: Falmer Press

James, A, Jenks, C and Prout, A (1998) *Theorizing Childhood.* Cambridge: Polity Press.

James, O (2002) *They F*** You Up: How to Survive Family Life.* Polmont: Bloomsbury

James, W (1890) *Principles of Psychology.* New York: Holt

Jenks, C (2000) Zeitgeist Research on Childhood. In Christensen, P and James, A (eds) *Research with Children. Perspectives and practices.* London: Routledge Falmer

John, M (2003) *Children's Rights and Power. Charging up for a new century.* London: Jessica Kingsley

Kahne, J (1996) The Politics of Self Esteem. *American Educational Research Journal.* 33 (1) p3-22

Kamler, B (1999) *Constructing gender and difference: critical research perspectives in early childhood.* Cresskill, N J: Hampton Press

Kantor, R, Elgas, P M, and Fernie, D E (1998) Cultural knowledge and social competence within a preschool peer-culture group. In Woodhead, M Faulkner, D and Littleton, E (eds) *Cultural Worlds of Early Childhood.* London: Routledge

Kearney, C (2003) *The Monkey's Mask: identity, memory, narrative and voice.* Stoke-on-Trent: Trentham

Kellett, M (2005) *How To Develop Children As Researchers: a step by step guide to teaching the research process.* London: Sage

Kelly, G (1955) *A Theory of Personality: The psychology of personal constructs.* New York: Norton

King, R (1984) The Man in the Wendy House. In Burgess, R (ed) *The Research Process in Educational Settings: ten case studies.* London: Falmer Press.

Kleinman, S and Copp, M (1993) *Emotions and Fieldwork.* Newbury Park, California: Sage.

Lacey, C (1970) *Hightown Grammar: the school as a social system.* Manchester: Manchester University Press

Laing, R D (1960) *The Divided Self: an existential study in sanity and madness.* Harmondsworth: Penguin

Langsted, O (1994) Looking at quality from the child's perspective, in Moss, P and Pence, A (eds) *Valuing Quality in Early Childhood Services.* London: Paul Chapman Publishers

Layard, R (2005) *Happiness: Lessons from a new science.* London and New York: Penguin

Layard, R and Dunn, J (2009) *A Good Childhood. Searching for values in a competitive age.* London: The Children's Society and Penguin Books

Lewis, A and Lindsay, G (eds) (1999) *Researching Children's Perspectives.* Buckingham: Open University Press.

Lewis, M and Brooks-Gunn, J (1979) *Social cognition and the acquisition of self.* New York: Plenum

Lewis, V, Kellett, M, Robinson, C, Fraser, A. and Ding, S (2004) *The Reality of Research with Children and Young People.* London: Sage.

Lindsay, G (2000) Researching Children's Perspectives: Ethical issues. In Lewis, A and Lindsay, G (eds) *Researching Children's Perspectives.* Buckingham: Open University Press

Lucey, H (2001) Working with Emotions. In Walkerdine V, Lucey H and Melody J (eds) *Growing Up Girl: psychosocial explorations of gender and class.* Basingstoke: Palgrave

Lucey, H and Reay, D (2000) Identities in transition: anxiety and excitement in the move to secondary school. *Oxford Review of Education,* 26, (2) p19 -205

MacLure, M and Jones, L (2009) *Becoming a Problem: How and why children acquire a reputation as 'naughty' in the earliest years at school. ESRC report* (RES-062-23-0105)

Marsh, H W (1992) Self Description Questionnaire (SDQ1): *A theoretical and empirical basis for the measurement of multiple dimensions of preadolescent self concept. A test manual and research monograph.* Macarthur, New South Wales, Australia, University of Western Sidney, Faculty of Education

Marsh, H W and Hattie, J (1996) Theoretical Perspectives on the Structure of the Self Concept. In Bracken, B (ed) *Handbook of Self Concept.* John Wiley and Sons

Maslow, A H (1954) *Motivation and Personality.* New York: Harper and Row

Mason, J (1996) *Qualitative Researching.* London, Thousand Oaks, California: Sage

Masten, A S and Shaffer, A (2006) How Families Matter in Child Development: Reflections from Research on Risk and Resilience in Clarke-Stewart, A and Dunn, J (eds) *Families Count. Effects on child and adolescent development.* New York: Cambridge University Press

Mayall, B (2000) Conversations with children: working with generational issues. In Christensen, P and James, A (eds) *Research with Children. Perspectives and practices.* London: Routledge Falmer

Maybin, J and Woodhead, M (2003) *Childhoods in Context.* Chichester UK: Wiley

McInerney, D M (2004) A discussion of future time perspective. *Educational Psychology Review.* 16(2) p141-151

McLaughlin, C with Alexander, E (2005) *Reframing personal, social and emotional education: relationships, agency and dialogue.* London: National Children's Bureau

Mead, G H (1934) *Mind, Self and Society.* Chicago and London: The University of Chicago Press

Measor, L and Woods, P (1984) *Changing Schools.* Milton Keynes: Open University Press

Miller, J B (1988) *Towards a New Psychology of Women.* London: Pelican

Morgan, D H (1981) Men, Masculinity and the Process of Sociological Enquiry. In Roberts, H (ed) *Doing Feminist Research.* London: Routledge and Kegan Paul

Morgan, R (2005) *Your Rights! Your Say. Younger Children's Views on Every Child Matters.* London: Commission for Social Care Inspection. www.rightsforme.org (January, 2009)

Moskovitz, S (1985) Longitudinal follow-up of child survivors of the Holocaust, *Journal of American Academy of Child Psychiatry* 22 (4) p401-7

Mosley, J (1996) *Quality Circle Time in the Primary Classroom.* Wisbech: Learning Development Association

Munro, P (1998) *Subject to Fiction: Women Teachers' Life History Narratives and the Cultural Politics of Resistance.* Buckingham: Open University Press

Noble, T and McGrath, H (2006-2009) *Bounce Back Resiliency programme,* http://bounceback.com.au/node/3 (December 2009)

Nutbrown, C (ed) (2002) *Research Studies in Early Childhood Education.* Stoke-on-Trent: Trentham

Oakley, A (1994) Women and children first and last: Parallels and differences between women's and children's studies. In Mayall, B (ed) *Children's Childhoods: observed and experienced.* London: Falmer

Oates, T (2009) Birthdate Effects – Summer-born children at a 'strong disadvantage. *Nursery World,* 15th Sept http://www.nurseryworld.co.uk/inDepth/898161/Analysis-Birthdate-Effects---Summer-born-children-strong-disadvantage/ (September 2009)

Oesterreich, L (1996) *Divorce matters: a child's view*, National Network for Child Care. Ames: Iowa State University

Oesterreich, L (1995) Biting hurts. In Oesterreich, L, Holt, B G and Karas, S (eds) *Iowa family child care handbook.* p239-242. Ames: Iowa State University http://www.nncc.org/Guidance/bit.hurt.html (February, 2009)

O'Kane, C (2000) The Development of Participatory Techniques: Facilitating children's views about decisions which affect them. In Christensen P and James A (eds) *Research with Children.* London: Routledge Falmer

Osborn, M, McNess E and Pollard, A (2006) Identity and transfer: a new focus for home-school knowledge exchange. *Educational Review.* 58 (4) p145-433

Paley Gussin,V (1984) *Boys and Girls. Superheroes in the Doll Corner.* Chicago: University of Chicago Press

Parten, M B (1932) Social Participation among Preschool Children. *Journal of Abnormal and Social Psychology.* 27 p243-269

Phelan, P (1993) *Unmarked. The politics of performance.* London: Routledge

Pollard, A (1987) Goodies, Jokers, and Gangs. In *Children and their Primary Schools.* London: Falmer Press

Pollard, A (2007) The Identity and Learning Programme: 'principled pragmatism' in a 12-year longitudinal ethnography. *Ethnography and Education,* 2, 1 p1-19

Pollard, A (2010) (ed) *Professionalism and Pedagogy: a contemporary opportunity,* a TLRP Commentary with GTCE. London: TLRP

Pollard, A with Anderson, J, Maddock, M, Swaffield, S, Warin, J and Warwick, P (2008) *Reflective Teaching 3rd edition.* London: Continuum

Pollard, A and Filer, A (1996) *The Social World of Children's Learning: case studies of pupils from 4 to 7.* London: Cassell

Pollard, A and Filer, A (1999) *The Social World of Pupil Career: strategic biographies through primary school.* London: Cassell

Pollard, A and Filer, A (2007) Learning, differentiation and strategic action in secondary education: analyses from the *British Journal of Sociology of Education.* 28 (4) p44-458

Pollard, A and James, M (2004) Personalised Learning: A commentary by the Teaching and Learning Research Programme. London: TLRP

Postman, N (1994) *The Disappearance of Childhood.* New York: Vintage Books

Power, S, Edwards, T, Whitty, G and Wigfall, V (2003) *Education and the Middle Class.* Buckingham: Open University Press

Prout, A (2000) Children's participation: control and self-realisation in British late modernity. *Children and Society.* 14, p304-315

Prout, A and James, A (1997) A new Paradigm for the sociology of childhood? Provenance, promise and problems. In James, A and Prout A (eds) *Constructing and re-constructing childhood: Contemporary issues in the sociological study of childhood.* London: Falmer Press.

Raphael Reed, L (1996) *Educational Research in Britain: Power and method.* Paper presented at BERA 1996 Lancaster University

Reay, D (2004) Gendering Bourdieu's concept of capitals? Emotional capital, women and social class. In Adkins, L and Skeggs, B (ed) *Feminism after Bourdieu.* Oxford: Blackwell

Roberts, H (1981) (ed) *Doing Feminist Research.* London: Routledge and Kegan Paul

Rogers, C (1982) *A Social Psychology of Schooling.* London: Routledge and Kegan Paul

Rogers, C R (1961) *On Becoming a Person: A Therapist's View of Psychotherapy.* London: Constable

Rogers, C R (1983) *Freedom to learn for the 80s.* Columbus: Charles Merrill

Rogoff, B (2003) *The Cultural Nature of Human Development.* New York: Oxford University Press

Rogoff, B, Paradise, R, Mejia Arauz, R, Correa-Ch´avez, M and Cathy Angelillo, C (2003) Firsthand learning through intent participation, *Annual Review of Psychology,* 54, p175-203

Rose, J (ed) (2009) *Independent Review of the Primary Curriculum.* London: Department for Children, Schools, and Families

Rose, N (1997) Assembling the modern self, in Porter, R (ed) *Rewriting the Self: histories from the renaissance to the present.* London and New York: Routledge

Rosenberg, M (1979) *Conceiving the self.* New York: Basic Books

Rosenthal, R and Jacobson, L (1968) *Pygmalion in the classroom.* New York: Holt, Rinehart and Winston

Ruddock, J and Flutter, J (2000) Pupil Participation and Pupil Perspective: 'carving a new order of experience', *Cambridge Journal of Education,* 30 (1) p75 – 89

Rutter, M (2002) Nature, Nurture, and Development: From Evangelism through Science toward Policy and Practice. *Child Development,* 73, 1, p1-21

Saldana, J (2003) *Longitudinal qualitative research: analyzing change through time.* Walnut Creek, Lanham, New York, Oxford: Altamira Press

Schaffer, H R (1996) *Social Development.* Oxford: Blackwell

Sedgwick, E K (1990) *Epistemology of the Closet.* Berkeley: University of California Press

Seligman, M E P (2002) *Authentic happiness; using the new positive psychology to realise your potential for lasting fulfilment.* New York: Free Press

Sherriff, N S (2007) Peer groups and social identity: an integrated approach to understanding masculinities. *British Educational Research Journal*, 33(3) p349-370

Shuayb, M and O'Donnell, S (2008) *Aims and values in Primary Education: England and other countries.* Interim Report. NFER, University of Cambridge and Esmee Fairburn.

Simons, J, Vansteenkiste, M, Lens, W and Lacante, M (2004) Placing motivation and future time perspective theory in a temporal perspective. *Educational Psychology Review.* 16(2) p121-139

Siraj-Blatchford, I, Clarke, K, and Needham, M (eds) (2007) *The team around the child: multi-agency working in the early years.* Stoke on Trent: Trentham

Skeggs, B (2004) *Class, Self, Culture.* London and New York: Routledge

Skelton, C (2001) *Schooling the Boys: Masculinities and Primary Education.* Buckingham: Open University Press

Sluckin, A (1981) *Growing up in the school playground: the social development of children.* London: Routledge and Kegan Paul

Smith, P (1986) Exploration, play and social development in boys and girls. In Hargreaves, D J and Colley, A M (eds) *The Psychology of Sex Roles.* London: Harper and Row

Social Exclusion Task Force (2007b), *Reaching Out: Think Family*, http://www. cabinetoffice.gov.uk/~/media/assets/www.cabinetoffice.gov.uk/social_exclusion_task_ force/think_families/think_families (August 2008)

Spender, D (1981) *Men's studies Modified: Impact of Feminism on the academic disciplines.* New York: Elsevier

Stanley, L and Wise, S (2002) *Breaking Out Again: feminist ontology and epistemology.* London: New York: Routledge

Stewart, I and Vaitilingam, R (eds) (2004) *Seven Ages of Man and Woman*, ESRC http://www.esrc.ac.uk/ESRCInfoCentre/Images/seven_ages_tcm6-5509.pdf (December 2009)

Suls, J and Sanders, G (1982) Self evaluation via social comparison: A developmental analysis. In Wheeler, L (ed) *Review of Personality and Social Psychology.* 3 p67-89. Beverley Hills: Sage

Sumison, J (1999) Critical Reflections on the Experiences of a Male Childhood Worker. *Gender and Education.* 11,4, p455-468.

Sure Start (2005) *The Birth to Three Matters Framework.* http://www.surestart.gov.uk/ resources/childcareworkers/birthtothreematters/ (4 July 2006).

Swain, J (2000) The money's good, the fame's good, the girls are good: The role of playground football in the construction of young boys' masculinity in a junior school. *British Journal of Sociology of Education,* 21(91) p95-109

Swann, W B (1990) To be adored or to be known: The interplay of self-enhancement and self-verification. In Sorrentino, R M and Higgins, E T (eds) *Motivation and Cognition.* 2 p408-448. New York: Guildford

Swann, W B, Pelham, B W and Krull, D S (1989) Agreeable fancy or disagreeable truth? Reconciling self-enhancement and self-verification. *Journal of Personality and Social Psychology.* 57 p782-791

Sylva, K, Roy, P, Painter, M (1980) *Child-watching at Playgroup and Nursery School.* London: Grant McIntyre

Tajfel, H and Turner, J (1979) An Integrative Theory of Intergroup Conflict. In Austin, W G and Worchel, S (eds) *The Social Psychology of Intergroup Relations.* Monterey, CA: Brooks-Cole

Thomas, R S *Children's Song poem,* http://www.poemhunter.com/poem/children-s-song/ (December 2009)

Thomson, R, Plumridge, L and Holland, J (2003) Longitudinal Qualitative Research: a developing methodology. *International Journal of Social Research Methodology: Theory and Practice,* 6, (3) p185 – 187.

Thorne, B (1993) *Gender Play. Girls and Boys in School.* Buckingham: Open University Press

Tizard, B and Hughes, M (1984) *Young Children Learning: talking and thinking at home and at school.* Glasgow: Fontana

Tizard, B (1991) Working mothers and the care of young children. In Woodhead, M, Light, P and Carr, R (eds) *Growing up in a Changing Society.* London and NY: Routledge

Toynbee, P and Walker, D (2008) *Unjust Rewards.* London: Granta

UNICEF (2007) *Child Poverty in Perspective: An overview of child wellbeing in rich countries,* Innocenti Report Card 7. Florence: Innocenti Research Centre

Vygotsky, L S (1991) Genesis of the higher mental functions. In Woodhead, M, Light, P and Sheldon S (eds) *Learning to Think: child development in social context.* London: Routledge

Walker, B and MacLure, M (2001) Home-school partnerships in practice. Paper presented at ESRC Sponsored Seminar Series *Parents and Schools: Diversity, Participation and Democracy,* UEA 20th June

Walkerdine, V (1981) Sex, power and pedagogy, *Screen Education,* 38 p14-24

Walkerdine, V, Lucey, H and Melody, J (2001) *Growing Up Girl: Psychosocial explorations of gender and class.* Basingstoke: Palgrave.

Warin, J (2007) Joined-up services for young children and their families: Papering over the cracks or re-constructing the foundations? *Children and Society,* 21 (2), p87-97

Warin, J, Maddock, M, Pell, A and Hargreaves, L (2006) Resolving identity dissonance through reflective and reflexive practice in teaching. *Reflective Practice.* 7(2) p231- 243

Warin, J, Solomon, Y and Lewis C (2007) Swapping stories, comparing plots: representing multiple perspectives in family interviews, *International Journal of Social Research Methodology: Theory and Practice,* 10, (2) p121-134

Warin, J and Dempster, S (2007) The salience of gender during the transition to Higher Education: male students' accounts of performed and authentic identities. *British Educational Research Journal*. 33 (6) p887-903

Warin, J and Muldoon, J (2009) Wanting to be 'known': re-defining self-awareness through an understanding of self-narration processes in educational transitions. *British Educational Research Journal*, 35(2), p289-303

Weare, K (2004) *Developing the Emotionally Literate School*. London: Sage

Whalley, M (2001) *Involving Parents in their Children's Learning*. London: Paul Chapman Publishing

Wheldall, K (1991) *Discipline in Schools. Psychological Perspectives on the Elton Report*. London: Routledge

Williams, F (2004) What matters is who works: Why every child matters to New Labour. Commentary on the DfES Green Paper 'Every Child Matters'. *Critical Social Policy*, 24(3) p406 – 427

Wolcott, H F (1994) *Transforming Qualitative Data: description, analysis and interpretation*. Thousand Oaks, California, London: Sage

Wolcott, H F (1999) *Ethnography: a way of seeing*. Walnut Creek, California: AltaMira press

Woodhead, M and Faulkner, D (2000) Subjects, Objects, or Participants? Dilemmas of Psychological Research with Children. In Christensen, P and James, A (eds) *Research with Children*. London: Routledge Falmer

Woodhead, M and Light, P (1991) *Child Development in a Social Context,* Open University Study Guide for E820. The Open University.

Yates, L and Mcleod, J (1996) 'And how would you describe yourself?' Researchers and researched in the first stages of a longitudinal research project. *Australian Journal of Education*, 40 (1), p88-103.

Yates, L and Mcleod, J (2006) How schooling, and particular schools, make a difference, Idiom, *Journal of the Victorian Association for the Teaching of English*, 42 (1), p7-14.

Young-Eisendrath, P (2009) *The Self-Esteem Trap: raising confident and compassionate kids in an age of self importance*. New York, Boston and London: Little, Brown and Company

Youniss, J (1980) *Parents and peers in social development*. Chicago: University of Chicago Press

Index